THE PARACHUTE

(*Henry M. Dittmer*)

THE PARACHUTE

from balloons to skydiving

by James R. Greenwood

New York: E. P. Dutton & Co., Inc.

FIRST EDITION

Published simultaneously in Canada by Clarke, Irwin
& Company Limited, Toronto and Vancouver.

Library of Congress Catalog Card Number: 64-10687

ACKNOWLEDGMENT

Quotation from "Renascence," by Edna St. Vincent Millay, is from *Collected Poems*, Harper & Row. Copyright
1912, 1940 by Edna St. Vincent Millay. By permission of
Norma Millay Ellis.

This book for my dear friend
Tiny Broadwick,
*a remarkable girl who pioneered
a trail few mortals dared to travel . . .*

PREFACE

Having plunged into space before, during and after World War II, I've watched with more than casual interest the rather amazing transition of premeditated parachute jumping from a form of death-defying exhibitionism to a well-regulated competitive sport.

I've also observed the growing acceptance of the parachute as the most practical, dependable method for escaping imperiled aircraft or landing a spaceship safely that man has yet contrived.

It is astonishing to realize that the parachute equipment used today, whether for sport, aerial emergencies, or warfare, looks and operates much like the old sacks with which a group of daredevils defied gravity in an earlier era.

There have been improvements in parachute materials and fabrication, just as there have been advances in other facets of aerospace technology. Nevertheless, the striking resemblance between modern parachutes and those of twenty, thirty, even fifty years ago, dramatically proves how farsighted the early parachutists were.

My purpose in writing this book is to give some of the basic information about parachutes and parachuting which ought to be understood by every beginner *before* he learns how to leap.

It is important that the novice know something about the development of the parachute, and of the men and women who, disregarding personal danger, gave parachuting status in the world of science. And he should know the equipment, regulations, clubs, competitions, training, and the costs of skydiving.

Above all, safety cannot be overstressed. Parachute jumping is hazardous; to deny any element of risk would be unforgivable.

Practiced under proper conditions, however, parachuting is no more dangerous than skiing, playing football, or climbing mountains. It does demand self-discipline, physical fitness, and better-than-average mental alertness. If the beginner possesses these qualities, and is willing to accept instruction and obey all the rules, he will find in this dynamic new space age sport an exhilarating enjoyment without equal.

But first a word of caution: Remember the adage, "It isn't the fall that hurts; it's the stop at the bottom." Wanting to jump is one thing; doing it is another. Posed at the exit door several thousand feet above the ground, the aspiring parachutist faces a critical moment of truth. He suddenly discovers that it is his decision, and only his.

Russ Gunby, former executive director of the Parachute Club of America, once put it this way: "Not everyone has the capability of becoming a safe sport parachutist . . . anymore than he has the capability of becoming a major league ball player, a race driver, or a prize fighter."

Parachuting is frequently called an obsession rather than a sport. But regardless of how you describe it, no other experience will ever come close to matching it.

CONTENTS

1   The Beginning   15

2   A Sport Emerges   37

3   Parachute Design   57

4   Learning to Leap   77

5   Advanced Skydiving   97

6   How Safe?   122

7   Champions and Showmen   144

8   Heritage   162

Acknowledgments

The story on the following pages is largely a condensation of information gathered from many sources. Therefore, I am indebted to many people for their generous help.

First of all, my special thanks to the prolific Martin Caidin, whose friendship and counsel I value so highly that very soon I hope to toss him out of an airplane, so that he, too, may taste the thrills of free flight through space.

My thanks to Louis Barr for introducing me to parachuting one frightening day in Alexandria, Virginia, and to Bob Ashburn, my pilot that first time out; to Keany Kopp, a fellow jumper with whom I worked in the long ago; to former associates Bevo Howard, Woody Edmondson, and Charlie Bing, for their compliments on my aerial displays.

My appreciation to Gene Guerny and Joe Skiera of the United States Air Force, for opening up historical files; the Pioneer Parachute Company's Herman Weber, Irving's Dave Gold, and Switlik's Dick Switlik; and to Russ Brinkley, a walking encyclopedia of barnstorming lore; and General Harold R. Harris, first to "hit the silk" from a falling plane . . .

Also to Bob Spatola, man behind the scenes at Orange in 1962; to America's two crack service demonstration teams and their public information officers, Tom Erickson of the Navy *Chuting Stars* and Will Goodrich of the

Army *Golden Knights*, and Will's predecessor, Doug Runnels; Lyle Cameron of *Sky Diver* and Ron Simmons of *Parachute*.

Many others were most helpful, among them skydivers Reyn White, Dave Burt, and Jim Garrison; Deke Sonnichsen, president of the Parachute Club of America; Ralph Whitener and Lou Davis of the National Aeronautic Association; and Phil Swatek, Jim Rudolph, and Marshall Benedict of the Federal Aviation Agency, along with Craig Lewis who has since left FAA . . .

Then there's Jae Greenberg, and Joe Christy, who handled my first book; and my colleagues in the craft— Pete Bulban, Bob Stanfield, Pete Bowers, George Haddaway, Dave Cooke, Don Downie, Max Karant, Ed Talbert, Jim Yarnell, and John Zimmerman, to name a few —whose heartwarming encouragement, enthusiastic support and professional guidance have assisted me immeasurably.

I am especially grateful to Joe Crane, one of the pioneers in international parachuting and founder of competitive jumping; and to my other flying-circus buddies of yesteryear, for richly vivid memories of low-level aerobatics, wing-walking, delayed jumps and cheering crowds—a colorful, romantic chapter in the incredible saga of aviation progress.

And thanks to my own dear Eloise, Roxanne, and Jeanne, for their devotion, inspiration and gentle understanding.

THE PARACHUTE

THE BEGINNING   1

LONG BEFORE MAN INVENTED A MACHINE CAPABLE OF defying the laws of gravity, and of propelling him through the oceans of air surrounding his planet, he had already devised a practical means of returning to earth with reasonable safety.

The word "parachute" derives from the Italian verb *parare* and the French noun *chute*, meaning "to guard against a fall." It is based on the principles that there are two forces acting upon a falling object. Gravity pulls it down, while the resistance of the air through which it falls tends to retard it. The parachute's broad, flat surface area increases the falling object's air resistance. This, in turn, counterbalances much of the strong gravitational pull and, consequently, slows the rate of fall.

Facts on the parachute's origin are scarce. Possibly it existed in the age of Icarus, the legendary Greek hero, symbol of man's earliest dreams to emulate the birds. If it did, Icarus didn't wear one. For as he flew higher and higher, heat from the sun's rays melted his wings of wax and he fell to his death in the sea.

There is a legend that Emperor Shih Huang Ti of China, who reigned from 221 to 207 B.C., enjoyed leaping from the newly completed Great Wall holding a large parasol.

There is some evidence that Chinese actors of the early fourteenth century used a crude umbrella-like apparatus to make spectacular entrances on theater stages. One thing is certain: the parachute is much older than the airplane, older even than the hot-air balloon, by at least several hundred years, if not several thousand.

Four hundred and fifty years ago, the ingenious Leonardo da Vinci designed a parachute that would allow a man to "fall from a great height without injury to himself." It was a pyramid-shaped contraption, not unlike a modern parachute, which he described as a "tent roof of calked linen twelve yards broad and as many yards high."

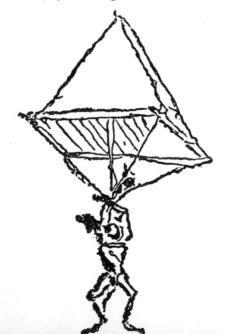

Leonardo da Vinci made this sketch of his parachute design about 1480. He called the parachute a "tent roof." (*Smithsonian Institution*)

Parachutes for escape
from high places
were described
in a book by
Fausto Veranzio, published
about 1600. One of
the illustrations is of this
model being tested.
(*Smithsonian Institution*)

Fausto Veranzio, another Italian obsessed with parachuting, built a square wooden framework covered with canvas in 1617. He planned to use it to test Da Vinci's theories by jumping from a tower in Venice, but the experiment never came off.

Two brothers, Joseph and Etienne Montgolfier, are known to have conducted parachute tests with animals nearly a decade before they became the first to develop a man-carrying balloon. Joseph Montgolfier, in 1777, successfully dispatched some sheep from a high tower by using parachutes seven feet in diameter. Five years later, the Montgolfiers made their famous ascent in their hot-air balloon.

On December 26, 1783, Sébastian Lenormand, a professor of physics and chemistry at Montpellier, France, risked his life to prove a theory. Credited with coining the word "parachute," Lenormand stepped off the tower of Montpellier Observatory wearing a canvas contrivance fourteen feet across. Landing hard but relatively unharmed, the fearless professor announced that he had just perfected a way of escaping from burning apartment houses.

Lenormand's invention had little appeal to tenants of tall buildings, however, but adventurous aeronauts tinkering with hot-air balloons saw in the parachute a great potential. As a result, the early balloonists became the early jumpers.

Thus, parachutes came into general use with ballooning. Not only did they provide a safety factor should the bag burst; they added new thrills for spectators witnessing balloon ascensions. The early balloon chutes swung freely from the bottom of the basket, suspended from its top or apex. The chute was released by severing a retaining cord. Instead of wearing a harness, the jumpers descended first in a basket, then later on a trapeze bar.

A professional showman, Jean-Pierre Blanchard, probably did more to popularize aerostation—the science of lighter-than-air flight—than any other balloonist of his day. And he also pioneered important advances in parachute construction.

Blanchard, in 1785, rose in a balloon of his own making that incorporated a parachute between the envelope and the basket. Believing the bag about to burst at 1,500 feet, he simply cut the ropes holding the basket and descended safely as the crowd cheered. His canopy, which measured 21 feet in diameter, can be compared to the modern emergency parachute of 24 feet.

Sometimes called the father of American aeronautics, Blanchard, in 1793, made the first balloon ascension in the United States under the auspices of President George Washington. He also released a dog, cat, and squirrel attached to a single chute from an altitude of several thousand feet. This was one of the first experiments with a parachute made of silk which could be folded. Until then, the cloth canopies were held open by a square or circular framework.

One of the most romantic figures in the pioneer days of parachuting was André Jacques Garnerin, who made his first drop over Paris on October 22, 1797. Garnerin, who had designed parachutes while serving a prison sentence in Budapest, soon won international recognition for his jumping feats in France and in England.

Garnerin's chute, made of wood covered with canvas, resembled a king-sized beach umbrella. His first design consisted of 870 square feet of cloth, about 75 square feet more than modern sport parachutes. Divided in 32 panels, the cone-shaped chute had a wooden disc at the apex. It was about 23 feet in diameter and weighed more than 100 pounds. Yet every parachute he developed oscillated so badly that Garnerin always got actively airsick on the way down. At the suggestion of an astronomer named

Lalande, Garnerin cut a hole in the top of the chute, allowing a stream of air to escape upward, instead of causing instability by curling under the sides. This dampened the swinging motion. Today almost all parachutes have a vent at the canopy apex.

Although Jean-Pierre Blanchard had elected to parachute from what appeared to him a faulty balloon, most aviation historians credit the Polish aeronaut Jordaki Kuparento with making the first recorded emergency jump on July 24, 1808. Kuparento, floating lazily in a clear summer sky, suddenly saw his hydrogen sphere burst into flames. He promptly cut himself loose and drifted slowly to earth under his open parachute.

Some aeronauts actually used their balloons as parachutes. In 1838, John Wise, the American exhibitionist, allowed his balloon to explode at 13,000 feet. Deflated, the limp fabric gathered at the top of its surrounding rope network to form a perfect parachute. Wise then descended safely, supported only by fragments of the damaged bag.

During the nineteenth century there were many bold aeronauts who defied gravity with balloon and parachute. One, an Englishman named Robert Cocking, gave his life trying to solve the stability problem. Cocking scored high on enthusiasm and courage but had little knowledge of physics.

He built a rig containing 124 square yards of Irish linen, which he rigidly braced with hoops and spars to hold it open in the shape of an inverted cone, with the peak at the bottom. The top measured 34 feet in diameter, and the entire apparatus weighed 223 pounds. One evening in July, 1837, he attached the bulky upside-down device to a balloon, ascending to 5,000 feet over London. Upon cutting himself loose, the whole thing collapsed. Cocking crashed to his death.

Though scientists paid little attention to it, parachuting continued to grow in popularity all over Europe and the United States. No one questioned its value as a circus attraction, and many jumping balloonists earned precarious livelihoods by thrilling thousands at fairs and carnivals.

Meanwhile, a few imaginative parachutists were experimenting with new materials and techniques. Perhaps the greatest advance came in 1880 when Captain Thomas Scott Baldwin, the American aeronaut, introduced a flexible, folded parachute which he stored in a bag on the side of his balloon basket. He also developed a body harness to which the parachute could be attached. It was connected to the canopy by shroud or suspension lines, quite similar to those of modern parachutes.

Baldwin was best known for his lighter-than-air work. He teamed with Glenn Hammond Curtiss to sell the United States Army its first dirigible in 1908. (Curtiss produced the motor power, Baldwin the balloon.)

While Italian and French parachutists contributed most to parachute progress in the early years, virtually all major developments after 1900 must be credited to the Americans, Germans, and British.

Pioneering efforts in the United States around the turn of the century were spearheaded by Baldwin and Charles Broadwick and A. Leo Stevens. In Germany, the enterprising, daring Kathe Paulus, who stuffed her canopy into a cloth sack that could be ripped open after she leaped, finally persuaded the German Air Force to adopt parachutes at the beginning of World War I. And in England, E. R. Calthrop worked tirelessly on his "Guardian Angel" design.

When, on December 17, 1903, the Wright brothers achieved the world's first powered flight in a heavier-than-air machine, Charles Broadwick immediately saw the parachute as a potential aerial life preserver.

Broadwick, a prominent aeronaut in his own right, realized that the parachutes then available, while safe for balloon jumping, would probably tear to shreds if opened at higher speeds. There was also danger of fouling the canopy or lines on some part of the airplane. That some aviator might be dragged to certain death in this way seemed a convincing argument against using the parachute with an airplane, but Broadwick and Stevens were certain the problems could be overcome.

To adapt the parachute to the flying machine, it would have to be packed in a relatively small container, constructed of much stronger fabrics than the cotton and linen material then generally used, and operated manually by the jumper after he cleared his stricken craft.

Working independently, Leo Stevens also developed a pack or container for the parachute, a ten-ounce piece of canvas cut in the shape of a fat cross. Rounded at the edges, the sides folded over the canopy; the pack was joined to a harness worn by the jumper. Stevens's greatest invention was the ripcord, a rather simple device that replaced the complicated series of interlocking pack closure strings and static line.

Stevens installed cones and grommets along the free edges of his parachute container flaps. When the flaps were folded over the canopy, the grommets—large metal eyelets—fitted over the upturned cones. A length of thin piano wire ran through small openings at the cone tips, which protruded above the grommets, locking the pack closed.

A short piece of rope, attached to the long end of the wire, looped over the jumper's shoulder, terminating in a ring lightly tacked to the parachute harness and easily accessible to the wearer's right hand. Moreover, strips of springy whalebone were embedded in the container flaps, thus ensuring faster, more positive openings. It was a very compact assembly; the entire pack, parachute and harness, weighed under 25 pounds.

To release the chute, the jumper, with pack strapped on his back, would clear the plane, then yank the ring or handle, withdrawing the piano wire. Immediately the container flaps, under combined pressures of the loosely packed canopy and the whalebone springs, burst open, ejecting the parachute into the air where it rapidly expanded. The whole opening process took about three seconds, almost as fast as today's models.

Because it takes two or three seconds for most parachutes to deploy and fully open, it is much safer to jump from altitudes of 1,000 feet or more. This was especially true in leaping out of slow-flying airplanes or balloons.

Stevens designed his parachute-opening mechanism in 1908, yet not until October, 1912, did anyone try it from an airplane. Arthur Lapham, strapped in a Stevens rig and with Harry B. Brown as pilot, bailed out of a Wright biplane at 4,000 feet. On May 20, 1913, Lapham jumped from 300 feet, and lived.

On June 21, 1913, Georgia "Tiny" Broadwick became the first woman to parachute from an airplane. Her pilot was Glenn L. Martin, who became one of the leaders in the aircraft industy. Tiny Broadwick used the new coat pack designed by her foster father, Charles Broadwick. It had a red, white, and blue canopy made of silk and linen, and the shroud, or suspension, lines were Italian hemp.

The Broadwick coat pack looked like a knapsack attached to a snug-fitting canvas jacket to which harness straps were stitched. It was the original back-type parachute in which harness and container formed a complete assembly. Broadwick advertised it as the "Patent Safety Pack Vest."

At first the Broadwick parachute deployed when the falling jumper's weight broke a connecting cord which had one end tied to the pack, the other end to the airplane. Later models were operated manually—the parachutist would pull the release cord himself, breaking strings holding the pack closed.

Tiny Broadwick demonstrates her method of leaping from Glenn L. Martin's biplane. She is wearing a new "coat pack" parachute made by her foster father, Charles Broadwick. The photograph was taken in 1913.

Tiny Broadwick used this model when she jumped for United States Army observers in 1914 at San Diego, California, at the first official demonstration of a parachute to the Federal government.

As a result of this successful test, the Army's aviation section ordered its first parachute—a Broadwick Patent Safety Vest—for further testing.

Three years earlier, stunt man Grant Morton, entertaining a seaside crowd at Venice, California, had dropped from a Wright biplane piloted by Frank Steitz. Morton, carrying his folded canopy in his arms, thus made the first parachute descent from an airplane. Military historians, however, claim the honor belongs to Captain Albert Berry, who jumped from a Benoist pusher flown by Tony Jannus at Jefferson Barracks, Missouri, in March, 1912—nearly a year later.

Berry's chute was packed in a metal cone fixed to the plane's underside. When ready to leap, he crawled down to the landing-gear axle, slipped into his harness, and let go. The weight of his falling body pulled the parachute out, but Berry dropped 500 feet before his canopy fully inflated.

On August 19, 1913, the famous French aviator Adolphe Pégoud made the first parachute jump from an

Pioneer parachutist Floyd Smith models the original Broadwick pack sold to the United States Army's young aviation section in 1914, after a successful exhibition by Tiny Broadwick. (*U.S. Air Force*)

airplane in Europe. To do it, he went up alone in a fine Blériot monoplane and purposely sacrificed his machine so that he might sample the thrills of parachuting. Drifting to earth under his open canopy, Pégoud watched in amazement as his pilotless Blériot executed fantastic gyrations while flying wildly out of control.

This experience gave Pégoud ideas for new aerobatic maneuvers, including the first complete loop ever tried in an airplane, which he executed several weeks later.

There were many successful jumps from planes in the next few years, but aviators still refused to wear parachutes. Most of the chutes then in existence were impossibly clumsy, or were too large, too heavy or unwieldy to be carried aloft in frail flying machines. The designs of Stevens and Broadwick were exceptions, but marketing them to pilots proved more of a merchandising chore than either inventor could manage.

Lincoln Beachey, one of the greatest exhibition pilots of all time, flew several jumpers in the years he performed aerobatics between 1910 and 1915. Yet he scoffed at parachutes. Had he been wearing one the day he stunted a new monoplane at San Francisco in 1915, he might have saved his life. The plane broke its wings at the bottom of a dive, and Beachey died.

World War I, which was to see so many aviation firsts, gave tremendous impetus to the development of parachutes. First to benefit were the crews who manned observation balloons. The sausage-shaped balloons were anchored to the ground and were filled with volatile

Most parachutes used for emergency jumps from combat observation balloons in World War I were the individual type worn by crewmen. But some designs, like this, lowered the basket of the balloon. (*U.S. Air Force*)

hydrogen gas. When struck by incendiary bullets, they would catch fire and explode.

Early in the war, the top end of the observer's parachute was attached to the balloon basket, the other end to his harness. In an emergency, the airman simply jumped over the side. Later balloons were equipped with chutes packed in conical containers secured outside the basket.

As the tactical and strategic use of aircraft increased, small parachute flares of magnesium, thrown from night bombers, were employed to illuminate targets; and under cover of darkness spies were dropped deep behind enemy lines to float silently down beneath their canopies of black material. However, fighter pilots still fought their aerial battles without parachutes.

Then, in 1917, the pilot of a French Nieuport riddled a German Fokker with a burst of machine-gun fire. Flames swept the Fokker as it twisted into a deadly spin. Suddenly the startled Frenchman saw his adversary scramble over the cockpit rim and fall away from the crippled Fokker. And almost as suddenly a huge white umbrella billowed out over the German's head, halting his mad plunge downward.

The German pilot had used a chute made by Otto Heinecke. It had been piled in a bucket built into the bottom of his plane, much like those used in observation balloons.

Heinecke improved his basic design, and soon German pilots were wearing back packs very similar to the Broadwick and Stevens models, though they still depended on a static line for the automatic opening. The French, British, and Americans were also working independently on parachute ideas. Individual designs varied little. Some were patterned after the Broadwick pack, some on the German type, and still others were slung under the airplane's fuselage.

By the end of the war in 1918, a high percentage of Allied pilots were wearing the British Mears or Guardian Angel, the French Ors or STA, or the American-made AEF parachute. And a number of Allied flyers, as well as balloonists, owed their lives to the thin threads of a parachute canopy.

Under the guidance of Floyd Smith, parachute experiments were in progress at McCook Field in Dayton,

Ohio, now part of Wright-Patterson Air Force Base. In 1919 the United States Army chose Major E. L. Hoffman to supervise further parachute development. Hoffman immediately assembled a team of experts, among them Floyd Smith, Guy M. Ball, James M. Russell, James J. Higgins, Ralph Bottriel, and a daring high diver named Leslie "Ski-Hi" Irvin.

Hoffman set out to perfect a foolproof, manually operated parachute pack. A design advanced by Smith, incorporating the best features of the Broadwick and Stevens models, ultimately evolved into United States Army Parachute "Type A" back pack, a vast improvement over previous equipment. It featured a silk canopy 26 feet in diameter, 32 shroud lines made of silk, a web harness, a puckered vent 48 inches in diameter, and a pilot chute.

On April 23, 1919, Leslie Irvin jumped from an Army DH-4 flown by Floyd Smith, successfully proving the Type-A pack in the first manned test of a free-type parachute. He leaped at 1,500 feet, pulled the opening cord, and the canopy blossomed almost at once above him.

Although elated by their success, Hoffman and his dedicated associates were determined to refine their initial product and evaluate others. Often risking their lives, the team of civilian and military engineers finally came up with the simplified United States Army Parachute "Type S"—the "S" for "service" model. It is the progenitor of all modern personnel parachutes, whether for emergency or for sport application.

The Type S measured 24 feet in diameter and had 24 shroud lines, each strong enough to support a load of 350 pounds. The silk canopy had a flatter shape; its puckered vent had been reduced from 48 to 18 inches across. From this basic design evolved seat, chest, and lap pack models, some types fixed to the harness, others arranged to attach quickly with heavy snaps.

By March, 1924, it had become mandatory for all Army and Navy aircrews to wear the standard Type-S parachute. Several McCook Field test pilots had saved their lives with parachutes. Among them, Lieutenant Harold R. Harris, on October 20, 1922, became the first flyer to escape a disabled airplane with a free-type, manually operated service pack.

Development work continued in the Army Air Service Engineering Division's parachute section, yet none of the radically new and different shapes that appeared from time to time was ever adopted for service use. Among other types tested, which eventually found their way into commercial production, at least on a limited scale, were the "Hoffman Triangle," the "Russell Lobe" designed by Jimmy Russell, and the Follmer and Clogg square chute.

The McCook Field team probably did more to advance parachute equipment and parachuting than anyone else. For his contributions to the science of flight and flying safety, Hoffman in 1927 received the coveted Collier Trophy.

Finally satisfied that his group had achieved a dependable, free-type service pack, Hoffman spent the

Forerunner of modern manually operated parachute was this United States Army "Type A" service model first jumped by Leslie Irvin in 1919. Its basic configuration has changed little. (*U.S. Air Force*)

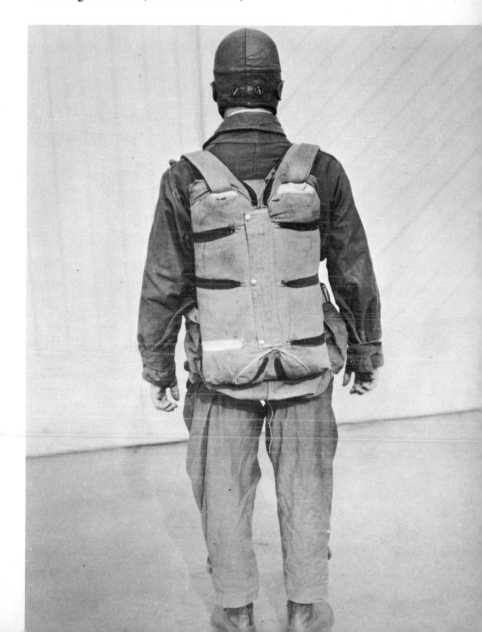

next few years attacking another problem—gigantic parachutes for airplanes. In 1927, Pilot R. Carl Oelze demonstrated Jimmy Russell's lobe chute. A Curtiss JN-4D
was lowered from 3,000 feet under a huge 50-foot lobe-
type chute anchored to the airplane's top wing at the
center of gravity.

The second pilot to demonstrate the parachute method
of landing a powerless aircraft safely was Colonel Roscoe
Turner, a noted speed flyer. At Santa Ana, California, in
April, 1929, Turner cut the switch of his Thunderbird
biplane 5,000 feet in the air, released a 60-foot Russell
chute, and floated to earth at the gentle rate of about 15
feet a second.

There were other tests, some successful, some complete failures. As late as 1940 Hoffman and his colleagues
still insisted that airplanes one day would mount huge
silken parasols for emergency use.

While airplane chutes were never adopted, canopies
as large and larger have dropped tanks, guns, bulldozers,
and other heavy equipment weighing upward of eight
tons. Some of these enormous umbrellas which saw action in World War II would cover three-quarters of an
acre. And in recent years every American astronaut,

E. L. Hoffman, who headed the United States
Army's original parachute test section at
McCook Field, was an advocate of huge
canopies capable of lowering enormous loads.
This is a 60-foot plane chute.

from suborbital pioneer Alan Shepard to the globe-gir-
dling Gordon Cooper, has watched a big parachute deploy above his Mercury spacecraft near the end of his
mission.

Originally conceived as a device for emergency evacu-
ation from high places, and later applied to circus exhibitions, parachutes today have a wide variety of uses
ranging from space-vehicle recovery systems to the
world's newest, most exciting participation sport called
skydiving.

A SPORT EMERGES 2

PARACHUTING GAINED NEW PRESTIGE ONE JUNE DAY IN 1963 when amateur jumper Valentina Tereshkova, a twenty-six-year-old former Soviet factory worker, became the first woman in space. Miss Tereshkova rode her Vostok VI spacecraft for 48 earth orbits in 71 hours. Near the end of her history-making mission, she bailed out and descended the last few thousand feet under a conventional parachute, landing about a quarter of a mile from her downed spaceship.

The significance of her feat is that Miss Tereshkova's chief qualification for space flight was experience in sport parachuting. She had 126 jumps in her logbook at the time of blast-off. Unlike the American astronauts, she was neither a pilot nor an engineer. The Soviet Union has led the world in popularizing parachute jumping as a sport and was the first nation to make use of parachute troops on a vast scale. This was not a new idea. Benjamin Franklin had recommended military chutes as early as 1784 when he asked this prophetic question:

The airborne trooper has been described often as the "world's finest fighting man," a contention his combat record supports. This jumper is a parachuting military-police infantryman. (*U.S. Army*)

"Where is the Prince who can afford so to cover his country with troops for the defense . . . as that ten thousand men descending from the clouds, might not, in many places, do an infinite amount of mischief before a force could be brought together to repel them?"

Later, Napoleon I considered invading England by having his soldiers jump from balloons which he figured could be propelled across the English Channel. And in October, 1918, Brigadier General William "Billy" Mitchell, an outspoken advocate of air power, conceived the tactical maneuver known today as vertical envelopment—landing paratroopers behind enemy lines. Had World War I lasted another few months, this might have been done.

But not until 1928 did General Mitchell have an opportunity to demonstrate his concept. At Kelly Field, Texas, he arranged for six Army infantrymen to jump from a Martin bomber, land, and set up a machine gun. The soldiers accomplished this within three minutes after touching down. The exercise gave birth to the "paratrooper," but most of the ranking American Army officers present were not overly impressed.

On the other hand, Russian and German observers who witnessed the Kelly Field drill went home convinced of the parachute's potential as an instrument of war. Soon parachuting was introduced in Russia as a national sport, and then incorporated into the Soviet Army. Russian parachutists participated in military maneuvers for the first time in August, 1930, at Voronezh.

Parachuting did not become a *mass* pastime in the Soviet Union until 1930, the year L. G. Minoff, a well-known pilot, began making exhibition jumps. About that time Minoff visited the United States to select a type of parachute best suited to the conditions prevailing in his country. He also advocated early instruction for beginners.

In 1933 Russia's all-union society for promoting aviation and antichemical defense, Osoaviakhim, established its first parachute *circle*. Toward the end of the same year it graduated 1,200 men and women. Then, in 1934, more than 4,500 jumped from airplanes, while countless thousands in all parts of the Soviet Union tried parachute descents from specially built towers. On their days off, many a Russian family in the mid-1930's found tower jumping exhilarating recreation.

By 1936 there were some 1,500 state-subsidized training towers and over 100 parachute stations in the Soviet Union. That year more than 21,000 free-fall sport parachute jumps were recorded, a number that continued to double each year until war broke out with Germany. Moscow's All-Union Parachute Center turned out instructors by the hundreds.

Professional competitive jumping was first seen in America in the 1920's. Contests for parachute-landing accuracy, better known then as "precision spot jumping," were featured events of major United States air meets in the 1920's, notably the old National Air Races. Cash prizes went to professional parachutists who in a series of jumps averaged the shortest distance from a landing circle.

Joe Crane, veteran exhibition jumper who still operates a commercial parachute service, is generally regarded as the father of competitive parachuting in the United States. As the free-type, manually operated parachute won greater acceptance, military and civilian jumpers discovered a new diversion—"slipping" their chutes toward predetermined landing areas.

Parachutist Ralph Wiggins does a drag-off from a biplane wing during an air show at Merced, California. Until the free fall became popular, this is the way most jumps started. (*Don Downie*)

At the 1926 National Air Races in Philadelphia, Joe Crane suggested that instead of a straight parachute exhibition, show officials stage a "spot-jumping" contest. Crane's idea was accepted, marking the first formal parachute competition.

The number of contestants at air meets gained steadily each year until management of parachute events became something of a problem. Unlike airplane pilots, jumpers during parachuting's early, formative years were not recognized by the Fédération Aéronautique Internationale, world governing body for aeronautical sport, or by the National Aeronautic Association, the United States representative of FAI. As a result, parachutists were second-class citizens at air shows.

Finally the NAA sanctioned an air meet at Roosevelt Field, Long Island, in October, 1933. Crane was given the job of organizing and supervising the spot-landing contest, which attracted 46 jumpers—14 more than had ever participated in any of the National Air Races up to that time.

Under Crane's expert direction, the parachute competitions came off without a hitch. William R. Enyart, then NAA executive secretary, left the Roosevelt Field meet with a new respect for parachuting as a sport. He called Crane to Washington late in 1933 so that NAA might establish procedures for issuing annual "sporting licenses" to parachutists, similar to those awarded pilots and balloonists. NAA also set up a parachute board, naming Crane as president.

The late Gene Rock, famed Indiana professional, set for exhibition leap from OX5-
powered Waco, circa 1930. His pilot is
Clarence Cornish. (*Bob McComb*)

That same year, Crane and his colleagues formed the
National Parachute Jumpers Association, to raise the
standards of professional exhibition jumping and to draft
basic rules in the interest of safety and showmanship.

However, compared with the rapid growth of parachuting abroad, few Americans would have anything to
do with it. Most people looked upon the parachutist as
some kind of nut, a reckless daredevil who would jump

at the pass of a hat. True, in the days of barnstorming flying circuses, the jumper was a rugged individualist. He had a leathery face, nerves of steel, and an obvious disdain for those who paid to watch him break his neck.

Membership in the National Parachute Jumpers Association barely reached two hundred by World War II. Meanwhile, as we have seen, parachuting had taken Russia by storm, winning a multitude of fans not only in large cities but also on hundreds of collective farms. Its popularity increased by leaps and bounds throughout Europe.

Germany had quickly grasped the value of parachute troops. In the 1930's, the Nazi high command worked feverishly to develop an effective military parachute organization as part of its plan for world conquest. At the outbreak of hostilities in 1939, both Russia and Germany parachuted troops in spearhead assaults in Finland and Poland. Finally, in 1940, the United States Army formed its first parachute test platoon of volunteers from the 29th Infantry.

The test platoon began training in New Jersey on parachute drop towers that had been used as a New York World's Fair attraction. On August 16, 1940, Private William N. King became the first enlisted man to

"Skilled, tough, ready around the clock!"—that's the motto of STRAC, the highly trained Strategic Army Corps which can deploy hundreds of airborne troops swiftly, effectively. (*Fairchild*)

jump as a United States Army paratrooper. Two weeks later, members of the original test unit made their first platoon mass jump.

Organized in November, 1940, the 501st Parachute Battalion became America's first parachuting combat unit. More airborne units were activated the following year. Then, in May, 1942, the United States Army Infantry Center at Fort Benning, Georgia, opened its famous parachute school. In its more than 20 years of operation, the Benning school has graduated over 200,000 paratroopers—and is still going strong.

From their first major battle jump in North Africa in World War II to their last in Vietnam, United States paratroopers have fought with a spirit, determination, and tenacity that have captured and held the imagination and respect of free peoples the world over.

The wartime demonstrations of parachutes in training, battle, and air operations gave impetus to jumping for sport. Following the fall of Japan in 1945, small groups of enthusiasts, mostly ex-paratroopers, formed the first regional jump clubs around the country. These combat-hardened airborne veterans saw in sport parachuting an exciting escape from the humdrum of peacetime pursuits.

After the war NPJA incorporated as the National Parachute Jumpers-Riggers, Inc., in order to admit licensed packers as well as jumpers. Proof of at least one jump or a parachute technician's certificate—civilian or military—was the only membership requirement.

During the 1930's Soviet jumpers were setting and breaking parachute records almost as fast as they could pull a ripcord. However, until 1948 no parachute records had ever been *officially* recognized. Largely through action of the National Aeronautic Association, the Fédération Aéronautique Internationale established a parachute category within its sporting code. FAI also created an International Parachuting Commission in 1948. Joe Cranc became its first United States delegate.

Today there are some 80 different classes of national and international parachuting records, plus rules and regulations governing FAI parachutist certificates, all record attempts, and world jumping competitions. And by 1952 NPJR had affiliated with NAA.

By 1949 the sport was very popular in France, where ten active parachute centers were subsidized by the government. Finally, in 1951, as an outgrowth of informal competitions for landing accuracy, sport parachuting catapulted into world prominence when the first international championships were conducted in Yugoslavia under FAI auspices. Five countries participated in the world meet.

France, top winner of the first contests, was host at the second international event at Saint-Yans in 1954. A single United States jumper, Fred Mason, carried the colors of NPJR. He competed alone against five-man teams from eight other nations, placing 21st in final standings. But his admirable effort sparked new interest in sport parachuting in the United States.

In 1950 a young naturalized American named Jacques André Istel went to Joe Crane for some advice on parachutes. Born in France, and scion of an international banking family, Istel had just earned his pilot's license. On his first long cross-country solo flight he crash-landed in a remote Illinois potato field, and decided he had better learn something about parachutes.

Crane soon had Istel jumping for fun at every opportunity. Then, in December, 1955, as Crane's emissary, along with Ray Young, an exhibition jumper, Istel represented the United States at the FAI International Parachuting Commission conference in Vienna. There rules were adopted for the third world meet (now a biennial event) to be held the following August in Moscow.

At the Vienna sessions Istel and Young saw a filmed report of the second international championships at Saint-Yans, which Russia had won. Istel made up his mind that the United States must at least match the other countries in number of contestants, if not in experience.

He journeyed from Vienna to Paris where the French national champion, Sam Chasak, taught him the rudiments of skydiving, a term that connotes the capability of stabilizing and maneuvering in free fall. This technique enables a jumper to control the attitude of his body during the delay before he opens his parachute. By proper execution, he may perform certain fundamental aerobatic figures somewhat like those of an airplane, such as turns, loops, and rolls.

The old theory that a man would lose consciousness if he delayed opening his parachute was exploded as early as 1922 when Lieutenant Harold R. Harris made the first emergency jump from an airplane. Bailing out of an experimental Loening fighter at 2,500 feet, Harris tumbled to within 500 feet of the ground before he found and pulled his ripcord. Landing uninjured, he had inadvertently proved that a jumper could fall free hundreds of feet without blacking out.

The first parachutist deliberately to subject himself to long-delayed openings was Sergeant Randall Bose, who in 1924 performed several free falls of 1,500 and 2,000 feet. But on one delay he ran into the deadly trap now known to all experienced free-fall parachutists—the flat spin.

The centrifugal force of rapid body rotation creates high G loads, causing a man to lose peripheral vision because of a pooling of the blood in the head and extremities. It is commonly referred to as "redout," and the jumper seems to see a curtain of redness before the eyes. It occurs when insufficient quantities of blood return to the heart and lungs to maintain adequately the oxygen-sensitive brain and eyes.

Constant spinning or any acceleration of rotational speeds prolongs the absence of critically needed oxygen in the brain. As a result, the brain "fails" and the jumper will pass out. Fortunately, Randall Bose opened his chute in time.

Steven Budreau, an Army parachute instructor at Self-

ridge Field, perhaps unknowingly first introduced the
fundamental principle of skydiving nearly forty years
ago. Early in 1925, Budreau leaped from a bomber at
7,000 feet to demonstrate that inherent perils of long
delays could be eliminated if the jumper stabilized himself during the free fall. Budreau fell free for more than
3,500 feet—under perfect body control—before pulling
his ripcord.

Another pioneering exponent of the controlled free
fall, H. E. "Spud" Manning, went Steve Budreau one
better. He would jump from 12,000 and 14,000 feet,
trailing flour as he fell. In 1932 he jumped from 16,665
feet and waited until he was within 1,400 feet of the
ground to crack his chute. In 43 seconds he had dropped
almost three miles. And by maneuvering the attitude of
his body, he attained a top speed of 225 miles per hour.

Jacques Istel returned home early in 1956, determined
to organize a regulation United States parachute team
and train it for the third world competitions in Moscow,
then a little more than six months away. He and Joe
Crane sent out invitations to fifty American professional
parachutists active in air shows. Next, Istel and Crane,
working through NPJR, screened the candidates, and
chose six men whom they considered to be the nation's
leading parachutists.

America's first official parachute team consisted of
Lewis B. Sanborn, an apprentice carpenter; George E.
Bosworth, sewing-machine operator; Lyle L. Hoffman,
an upholsterer; Walter R. Fair, signpainter; Floyd M.

Hobby, auto mechanic; and George J. Stone, a steeplejack. Istel acted as team captain.

Each jumper came from widely scattered sections of the United States and paid his own way to training headquarters in Trenton, New Jersey. And though all were accomplished spot jumpers, each man realized he needed a lot of work to become adept at the finer points of skydiving. From dawn to dusk the team went through a rigid, rugged routine—a jump, criticisms, suggestions, then another jump. Evenings were spent packing chutes.

On the way to Moscow the team stopped off at the French parachute station at Brisacrosse, the Centre Nationale de Parachutisme. There the Americans hoped to polish their jumping style with the help of French experts, but bad weather set in, and they were unable to make more than a few jumps.

Czechoslovakia accumulated the highest total point score to win the 1956 international parachuting championship. Other participating nations finished in this order: Russia, Bulgaria, France, Yugoslavia, United States, Poland, Romania, Hungary, and Israel. While disappointed over the outcome, Istel nevertheless felt the Americans had done well under the circumstances.

Istel now quit his job with a Wall Street investment firm to devote all his time to spreading the gospel of sport parachuting throughout the United States. As the Istel crusade gained momentum in 1957, NPJR changed its name to the Parachute Club of America.

Also in 1957, Istel and Lew Sanborn, high point scorer

for the United States at Moscow, founded Parachutes, Incorporated, a commercial concern offering equipment sales, service, rentals and jumping instruction. It operates two sport-parachuting centers, one at Orange, Massachusetts, the other at Lakewood, New Jersey. In 1958, the United States Army, after retaining Istel to train a select group of military jumpers in free-fall techniques, authorized interested personnel to engage in the sport.

As PCA membership grew, small local affiliate clubs began springing up around the country. Groups of enthusiasts were also formed in colleges and universities and in the three branches of the armed forces—Army, Navy, and Air Force.

Eliminations to select the 1958 United States parachute team were held at Abbotsford, Canada. Six civilians and one Army jumper qualified. Captained by Lew Sanborn, the United States team ended in sixth place out of fourteen nations represented in the fourth world sport-parachuting championships conducted in Bratislava, Czechoslovakia. Istel was high point scorer for the United States.

Highly proficient military jumpers now began winning important laurels for the United States. In the Adriatic Cup invitational meet at Tivat, Yugoslavia, in 1959, a United States Army team edged out Soviet Russia as it placed second in another 14-nation field. Loy B. Brydon, a private first class, scored second in overall point standings to achieve the best individual performance by an American skydiver up to that time.

In tryouts for the 1960 United States parachute team held at Fort Bragg, North Carolina, military jumpers swept the top eleven places. As a result, an all-Army squad represented the United States in the fifth biennial international championships staged at Sofiya, Bulgaria.

The United States team ended up fourth in the 1960 world meet, but young James Arender won first place in the style event, thus capturing America's first gold medal. And the following year, in the invitational contests at La Ferté-Gaucher, France, the official United States Army parachute team took all five first-place trophies finally to topple a long-standing Iron Curtain monopoly of sport parachuting.

At the sixth international parachuting championships, with the United States as host in August, 1962, at Orange, Massachusetts, the American team of civilian and military jumpers made their finest showing to date in world competition. United States parachutists won first place in three out of four categories and second in the fourth category. Jim Arender, now a civilian, emerged as individual men's parachuting champion of the world. An attractive California housewife and mother named Muriel Simbro walked off with similar honors in the women's division.

In 1963, the United States parachute team, composed of Army jumpers Phillip Vander Weg, Richard Fortenberry, Gerald Bourquin, Coy McDonald, and alternate Joe Norman, scored a decisive first-place victory in the European Cup Meet at Leutkirch, Germany. Some two

"The wonderful world of skydiving"—international champion Jim Arender falls at 120 miles per hour in a stable-spread position over Taft, California. (*Robert H. Buquor*)

months later, members of the 1962 United States men's and women's teams turned in a near perfect performance in the 1963 Adriatic Cup invitationals at Portoroz, Yugoslavia. They won nine first places out of a possible thirteen.

There were fewer than two hundred sports jumps in the entire United States in 1956, the year before the National Parachute Jumpers-Riggers became the Parachute Club of America. In 1963 the total number soared to an estimated fifty thousand.

Ranks of PCA have swelled from a handful of members in 1957 to more than 7,500 in 1963, roughly 50 per cent of all the active sport jumpers in America. Darrell C. "Deke" Sonnichsen, PCA president and 1962 United States team leader, has forecast that at its present growth rate, club membership will reach 35,000 by 1970. Impressive as this number might be, it is still but a fraction of the hundreds of thousands of men and women who are actively participating in the sport throughout the world.

Deke Sonnichsen stresses that PCA puts *safety* first. Club efforts are aimed at making modern parachuting a safe, sane recreational activity, and achieving for skydiving public recognition and acceptance as a popular sport.

The Parachute Club of America lists these main objectives: promote safety in parachuting; encourage unity among all participants; sanction competitions; document officially all record attempts; further education in the field of parachuting; cooperate with all aeronautical agencies; test parachuting equipment; compile, edit, publish, and disseminate information on the sport; select and train United States parachuting teams, and issue and validate parachuting licenses.

A nonprofit organization supported only by membership dues and fees, PCA, as a division of the National Aeronautic Association, supervises and monitors all sanctioned sport parachuting in the United States. Though its rigid safety rules have reduced the hazards of jumping to a minimum, to say there is no risk is like saying there's no danger in handling a loaded gun.

Once rejected by airmen as unsafe and impractical, the parachute has finally come into its own. If present trends continue, skydiving may eventually become one of this nation's leading competitive sports.

PARACHUTE DESIGN

It is estimated that during World War I about 800 airmen—balloonists, pilots, and observers—saved their lives with parachutes. Since then about 100,000 flyers are believed to have qualified for membership in the "Caterpillar Club," an informal organization of persons who used their parachutes in an aerial emergency.

Actually, there are less than 40,000 names listed on Caterpillar rolls, for many people never got around to registering their lifesaving leaps. Club records date from July 21, 1919, the day airship mechanic Henry Wacker and pilot John A. Boettner made the first emergency jumps in the United States.

Wacker and Boettner bailed out of the Goodyear sightseeing blimp *Wingfoot Express* as it burst into flames over the heart of downtown Chicago.

First of the famous Goodyear line of nonrigid airships, the *Wingfoot Express* had just been completed. Following a short test flight, Boettner welcomed aboard his first passengers, who had been selected from a long waiting list, staff photographer M. G. Norton and writer Earl Davenport of the Chicago *Herald and Examiner*. Also aboard was mechanic Carl Weaver.

Boettner ordered each man to put on a harness attached to individual balloon-type chutes rigged on the sides of the open gondola. The passengers did so rather reluctantly, commenting that if anything went wrong, they'd ride the craft down before trusting one of those confounded cloth contraptions.

As the big, ungainly bag cruised along over Chicago's loop district, Norton snapped pictures and Davenport scribbled notes. Wacker and Weaver listened to the ship's two air-cooled engines, each rated at 75 horsepower, which pulled the new pride of Goodyear through the skies at a leisurely 40 miles an hour. Suddenly the ship lurched drunkenly; static electricity had fired the envelope's highly inflammable hydrogen gas.

"Jump!" shouted Pilot Boettner. First Norton tumbled over the side, followed by Davenport, Wacker, Boettner, and Weaver. Davenport's parachute, hopelessly tangled, never opened. Weaver's canopy inflated, but ignited and burned up. Norton, within grasp of safety, was dashed against Western Union's building, breaking his legs. He then fell into the street, and died.

Only Wacker and Boettner survived. Tragically, blazing gasoline and wreckage crashed through a skylight of the Illinois Savings Bank on LaSalle Street, spreading death and destruction all over the main floor. Ten persons inside the bank, employees and customers, were killed.

Many others were seriously hurt. When the wave of hysteria that followed the horrifying disaster eventually subsided, Goodyear continued its airship program, using nonflammable helium instead of hydrogen.

Among other distinguished Caterpillars is Charles Lindbergh, who saved his life with a parachute on four different occasions, twice while flying the mail. Lindbergh also made about twenty exhibition jumps as a barnstormer, a few years before his famous nonstop solo flight to Paris in 1927. Another noted member is James H. "Jimmy" Doolittle, pioneer speed and stunt pilot, who led the historic B-25 bombing attack on Japan in April, 1942.

The Caterpillar Club got its name from the lowly worm which produced the silk used for so many years in parachute manufacture. Very early parachutes were constructed of cotton or linen, but eventually these fabrics were replaced by Japanese habutai silk. Habutai silk remained the standard parachute material until World War II.

There were several reasons for using silk in making chutes. It has great strength for its weight; it can be packed in a small space; it has a "springiness" that permits it to unfold and separate easily, and it has the ability to resist flames. It is vulnerable to moisture, vermin, oils and acids, however.

When war with Japan cut off the silk supply, accelerated parachute production rapidly consumed United States inventories. Needing a suitable substitute, nylon

was selected as the best of several synthetic fibers. Now used almost exclusively in American-made parachutes, nylon in many ways is superior to silk. But, like silk, it requires careful handling and proper storage. Foreign substances, such as salt water, grease, and ammonia, are harmful to it and could cause rapid deterioration. Fire will melt nylon.

Nylon doesn't have quite the elasticity of silk, yet it is more porous. Porosity enables a fabric to "breathe," or allow air to permeate its texture. This is vitally important to parachute operation and length of service. Whether built of nylon or silk, chutes stored or inactive for any length of time should be hung in drying towers and thoroughly aired for at least twenty-four hours before repacking. Canopies left in a packed condition for extended periods tend to develop permanent wrinkles in their folds.

Modern parachutes have many applications they are used for saving life, delivering weapons, slowing down landing jet aircraft, recovering space vehicles, dropping emergency supplies, fighting forest fires, and now for skydiving.

A unique photograph taken by Jim Meads near London on September 13, 1962, shows De Havilland test pilot George Aird ejecting from his crippled English Electric Lightning jet fighter 150 feet from the ground. Aird fell in the greenhouse at the left of trees and lived to fly again.

The primary function of the parachute is to resist the crushing forces of gravity, or, as in the case of high-performance jets, to brake the swift forward momentum of heavy winged craft on their critical landing roll. While dimensions, construction, and methods of deployment may vary according to a particular mission or purpose, all parachute configurations and systems are generally similar.

In contrast to the highly efficient, reliable, meticulously engineered equipment available today, the crude, bulky, claptrap rigs of the balloon era were little more than bundles of cloth, rope, and splintered wood. It's a wonder the attrition rate among pioneering aeronauts wasn't any higher.

Parachute development had made considerable progress by the time Major E. L. Hoffman received his orders to form an experimental unit at McCook Field. At least it had advanced somewhat beyond Captain P. A. Van Tassell's primitive paraphernalia of the 1880's. Van Tassell deserves to share with Captain Tom Baldwin much of the credit for creating a collapsible parachute.

By modern standards, Van Tassell's first parachute was intolerably weak. It was no more than a disc of canvas, perfectly flat if laid on the ground. To its edges were sewn hemp cords which connected to a square trapeze consisting of four bars. The cord lines, each about 15 feet in length, anchored to the upper sides of the four bars, which were so arranged as to form a "nesting" place for the jumper during his descent.

Despite its flimsy appearance, the Van Tassell concept was a step forward. Its unique design was a radical departure from the rigid apparatus then in general use. Van Tassell shrewdly and correctly concluded that, if properly introduced into the canopy, air pressure would not only sustain the parachute but blow it open as well.

His recognition of a simple natural law did away with complicated and burdensome brace structures—the special framework built to hold the canopy open at all times.

Several events occurred at McCook Field in the days right after World War I which had a profound influence on parachute design and acceptance. The first involved the unfortunate death of Lieutenant R. A. Caldwell of the Royal Air Force. He came to McCook in 1919 to demonstrate the British "Guardian Angel" attached-type parachute, though Leslie Irvin had already proved Floyd Smith's new free operating model in his historic jump some ninety days earlier.

Caldwell was determined to show Major Hoffman's test group that his parachute was adequate for all emergencies. It differed little from the balloon chutes; the parachute pack was attached to the bottom of the airplane fuselage, and a heavy line, which ran over the side of the cockpit, connected to a harness worn by the pilot.

Taken aloft in a DH, Caldwell dropped over the side. His plunging figure, like a body at the end of a hangman's rope, suddenly halted, snapped convulsively under the fuselage, swung frantically, then hurtled earthward.

The shroud lines of H.T. Smith's balloon-type parachute harness were attached to an automobile steering wheel. Smith used this rig between 1928 and 1935.

Streaming behind him were a few strands of hemp, futilely lashing the air. The attachment line had caught on an elevator post, breaking it clean. Falling with only his harness, he was killed instantly.

The value of the new manually operated service model was again driven forcibly home in 1920 when exhibition jumper William O'Conner used one to save his life. O'Conner worked for parachute designer LeRoy B. Jahn, who arrived at McCook with the prototype of a new model.

Jahn's creation featured four springs, each about four feet long, sewn into the canopy skirt. But before the Army examining board would permit a test jump, it ordered O'Conner to attach a reserve parachute to the front of his harness. Reluctantly, the jumper consented. He went to 2,000 feet in a USD-9 aircraft, leaped, and pulled the new Jahn pack open. The canopy deployed, flapped madly, but failed to inflate. It was hopelessly fouled, the spring entangled within the canopy folds.

O'Conner fought to trap air in his streaming parachute for more than 1,000 feet. Giving up, he cracked his reserve, which functioned perfectly. He landed safely with a parachute built by Major Hoffman, Smith, Irvin, and associates.

The death of Lieutenant Frederick W. Niedemeyer in 1921 resulted in the first official order directing Army flyers to wear parachutes. Niedemeyer, one of the few test pilots willing to endure parachutes before they became mandatory, went up without his pack one day because with it he couldn't sit comfortably in the small Fokker D-VIII he planned to fly.

While maneuvering the Fokker overhead, a wing ripped off and the plane fell into an uncontrollable spin. Niedemeyer had time to jump, but his parachute was in the hangar. Colonel Thurman H. Bane, then McCook Field commander, who witnessed the fatal accident, promptly ordered that parachutes from then on would be standard equipment for all airmen in his command.

Charged with developing a safe emergency parachute, Major Hoffman and his staff in 1919 established these objectives:

1. It must be lightweight, compact, and so carried as to offer minimum inconvenience and interference with the control of the aircraft.
2. It must be fast and positive in opening.
3. It must be secured to the wearer in a comfortable manner, which in no way would impede his leaving the aircraft.
4. It must be so packed and released that it does not open until the jumper has cleared the aircraft; a free type, manually operated.
5. It must have a releasing device that is simple, rugged, and sufficiently protected to withstand normal operational abuse.
6. It must be so packed that on its release the shroud lines cannot become entangled (the reason for hesitator loops).

7. It must be so designed that, on opening, the sudden stresses would be relieved. (This would be accomplished by a variable air vent at the canopy apex and the material's own porosity, thus reducing the danger of bursting panels.)

8. It must have a harness that can be fitted to any probable wearer.

9. It must have a harness strong enough to withstand stresses of violent opening shocks, and one so designed as to distribute these stresses to the wearer without injury. (For many years linen was considered the best material for harness construction.)

10. It must have a harness so disposed and attached to the wearer that regardless of his attitude when the parachute opens, he is in no danger of falling out.

11. It must be so designed as to eliminate excessive oscillations. (Another reason for the vent opening at the peak which, together with the fabric's permeability, permits excess air to escape.)

12. It must be designed so that the rate of descent is low enough to prevent injury to the wearer when landing. (Hoffman's group set 450 square feet as the minimum area of resistance for a standard canopy. Under inflation, a service chute 24 feet in diameter actually has a projected diameter of about 16 feet and a half, which will lower a 190-pound load at approximately 20 feet per second.)

13. It must have a harness which can be removed quickly and easily. (The conventional harness has three connections. Sitting in a sling position, the wearer can unfasten all three snaps without falling out of his harness.)

14. It must be so designed that repacking can be done readily.

15. It must be fabricated of a material which is not susceptible to flame propagation. (Silk had already been selected because it met this requirement, in addition to being strong.)

Army parachute engineers under Hoffman's leadership worked to improve the early Type-A pack, ultimately producing the Type S. The new model embodied all the best features of equipment developed by Baldwin, Broadwick, Stevens, and Smith, as well as the advanced innovations perfected by the McCook Field team.

Later military service pack specifications called for the "follow-through" theory of manufacture, a design principle based on the relative ruggedness of the various materials used in the parachute's construction—fabric, hardware, shroud lines, and webbing. The purpose is to bring the tensile strengths of all components to a ratio of one.

Except for refinements such as new fabrication techniques and new materials, the man-carrying parachute has changed little in the last forty-five years. Its basic design and mode of operation today are the same as the Army Type S.

There are different types and styles of personnel parachutes, such as the seat, lap, chest, back, and chair packs. The diameter of canopies will range from 22 feet to 32 feet, depending upon whether the equipment is designed for emergency, sport, combat, or auxiliary training use. Fundamentally, all parachutes are similar; therefore, the following description of the structure is that of a popular back model worn by skydivers.

The modern parachute has five major components— the pilot chute, canopy, suspension lines, harness, and container. Pilot chutes are small parachutes, normally requiring about one square yard of nylon cloth cut into panels, then sewn together and attached to a spring arrangement. Their own short suspension lines connect to the main canopy's apex.

Generally, canopies used for sport parachuting measure 28 feet in diameter. Called a "sail" by old-time parachutists, the 28-foot canopy comprises about 796 square feet of nylon fabric. The material itself weighs around one and a half ounces per square yard.

There are three basic styles of canopies in use today— the flat circular, the parabolic, and the conical types. Flat circular canopies are the most widely used in sport jumping. The parabolic models are designed primarily for military paratroopers. Conical chutes, on the other hand, have unique advantages for high-speed emergency escape systems.

A member of the United States Navy Chuting Stars team hurtles earthward. His trail is marked by colored smoke that pours from a canister attached to his right foot. (*U.S. Navy*)

The 28-foot sport canopy is a nylon polygon of 28 sides. It is made by sewing 28 gores together, which produces the umbrella shape. Gores resemble long triangular sections, like pie slices. Each gore wedge consists of four panels, joined by diagonal seams at a 45-degree angle to the gore center line. This bias construction provides maximum strength and elasticity.

The bottom, or outer, edge of the canopy is called the skirt or periphery; the top is known as the crown or peak, and has an elastic vent collar at the apex. This puckered vent (many chutes have an open vent and no collar) stretches to a diameter of about 18 inches when the canopy inflates, which relieves internal pressures and dampens oscillation during the descent. The skirt and vent hems are reinforced with nylon strips one inch wide, similar in appearance to surgeon's tape.

In the manufacture of parachute canopies, only top-grade nylon fabrics, with textures of the finest quality, are used. As a rule, the nylon material has a tensile strength of about 50 pounds per square inch—about 10 pounds stronger than silk fabric used in prewar chutes.

One of the major differences between sport models and the standard service-type parachute is the canopy. Skydivers jump modified canopies to enhance their steering capabilities. Whole gores and panels are cut out of the canopy, giving it an appearance of having been badly torn or ripped.

Some veteran skydivers design their own canopies, but only a master parachute rigger certificated by the Federal

Aviation Agency may actually make alterations or modifications.

In the so-called "blank gore" canopy, almost an entire gore is eliminated. In fact, many types have two complete gores missing; still others have additional panels around the skirt or individual sections removed to increase maneuverability. A few years ago sport jumpers used the two-slit Derry parachute, which Frank Derry designed in 1941. It featured canopy slits cut along two lines, then reinforced. The slits could be fully opened for forward speed or closed for straight vertical descent.

Modified parachutes work on the basic principle of jet propulsion. Air trapped under the inflated canopy is forced out through these openings behind the jumper, enabling him to travel a horizontal as well as a vertical path. He guides the descent by pulling on two "toggle," or control, lines that turn the canopy left or right, pointing him in the desired direction.

One might think that with huge sections cut out of a canopy, the jumper would drop like the proverbial ton of bricks. Not so. That a large canopy area is missing really doesn't affect the rate of descent to any appreciable degree, although there is naturally a limit to the number of panels or gores that can be safely removed.

Shroud lines, also called suspension lines, are made of nylon cords sheathed in a loosely woven nylon jacket or covering. Each shroud line runs continuously from one lower connector link up through the canopy to the apex, then down the other side of the canopy, terminating at another lower connector link.

The lines are encased in the canopy's radial or main seams—channels formed by stitching. They are sewn to the canopy only at skirt and vent seams. It takes about 75 feet of line to make the connection from link to link. There are 14 complete shroud, or suspension, lines which double over the canopy for a total of 28.

Secured in groups of seven to each of the four connector links, the shroud lines tie the canopy to the harness, a series of nylon webbing strips arranged to encircle the parachutist's shoulders, back, legs, and chest.

Harness straps form a weblike sling in which the jumper may sit or swing during his descent without danger of falling out. Elements of a standard harness include four lift webs, or risers (to which the shroud lines are attached by the connector links), the main sling, and the leg straps. The main sling has straps crossing the shoulders, chest, and back.

Harness webbing is exceptionally rugged, having a tensile strength of up to 5,000 pounds. Some harnesses are quite supple; others are stiff, depending upon the type of weave. Harness hardware consists of the shroud-line connector links, snaps, and the adapters for quick adjustment to size. There are from 16 to 20 metal parts in all.

Most of the sport harnesses on the market today are three-point attachment types, with connection snaps for two leg straps and one chest strap, as in the early service models. Comfortable and form-fitting, they are easily adaptable to the individual wearer. Some have quick-release lift webs hooked to the harness by ejector snaps that lock in place. To release the canopy after landing, the jumper merely unsnaps the ejectors.

The pack container is just what the name implies—it contains or houses the folded canopy, suspension lines, and pilot chute. Its primary purpose is to protect and hold in place until release all other parts of the parachute assembly except the harness itself. Tough and durable, most containers are made of either canvas or nylon, and are machine-stitched.

Components of the container include shroud-line retainers (hesitator loops—rubber bands or small strips of tape), harness keepers, opening bands, lift web slots, pack wing flaps, and the grommets and locking cones through which ripcord pins are inserted. Most sport parachutes are adaptable to either a static line for automatic opening or to the manually operated ripcord.

A flexible metal tube that secures to both harness and the container pack houses the free-type ripcord cable. The ripcord handle, sometimes called a D-ring, fits in a pocket sewn to the harness. It normally is located a few inches down from the left shoulder, though some jumpers prefer it on the right.

Unless a sleeve is used (sleeves will be discussed later), the shroud lines are stowed in a zigzag manner in the back or bottom of the container tray. They are held in place by their retainers—rubber band or nylon hesitator loops—to prevent the lines from slipping while the parachute is packed for storage or wearing. When the jumper activates his parachute, the lines pull free of these loops or bands.

As with back packs, there are several different types of reserve (for emergencies in training or sport jumping) parachutes available. Sport parachutists and others who make premeditated jumps are required by Federal law to wear two chutes—a main pack and a reserve or auxiliary parachute. The reserve is worn in front, fastened to quick-attachment rings or snaps about chesthigh on the main chute's harness webbing. It is used if the main parachute does not function.

Reserve canopies are usually 24 feet in diameter, although some older models are 22 feet. They fit into a smaller pack, have short ripcords, and will attach to any harness equipped for sport or training operations.

Some sport parachutists adapt automatic opening devices to their reserves. These are generally set to release the auxiliary canopy at 1,000 feet above the ground. This is an extra measure of safety should the jumper for some reason fail to open his main *or* reserve pack manually. Several lives might have been saved over the past few years if the unlucky jumpers had been wearing auxiliary chutes equipped with automatic openers.

Automatic opening devices operate barometrically or by a special timer. All military crews of high-performance aircraft wear chutes that will open automatically.

The reserve pack also serves as a platform for mounting the skydiver's instrument panel, which generally consists of an airplane-type altimeter and a stop watch. These instruments are used for instant altitude reference. The arrangement in no way interferes with the normal operation of the reserve parachute.

Now in general use by most sport parachutists is the deployment, or launching, sleeve, often erroneously described as a new innovation. The principle actually dates back to about 1940 when several exhibition jumpers built them to slow the process of main canopy openings.

Detached and stretched out on the ground, the deployment, or launching, sleeve looks like a limp, elongated windsock. It is drawn over the canopy, which has already been folded lengthwise, in a way similar to putting on a stocking. As a snug cover, it inhibits rapid inflation, holding the canopy together until the jumper is drawn upright. This tends to eliminate the eye-popping "snatch forces" and to reduce opening shock.

Use of deployment sleeves also prevents the possibility of fouling the main chute in the plane's tail group or having the jumper tangle in his own lines during the opening. However, the sleeve does increase the danger of one or more shroud lines slipping over the canopy before inflation.

The modern free-type, manually operated parachute is in all respects one of the most infallible mechanical devices ever contrived. Malfunctions are extremely rare; those that occur are usually the result of faulty rigging or improper jumping procedure on the part of the parachutist.

The hundreds of thousands of safe descents made in training, emergencies, combat, air shows, and in the new sport of skydiving attest to the parachute's high level of reliability.

LEARNING TO LEAP   4

WHAT MOTIVATES A MAN TO PLUNGE INTENTIONALLY into space and let his life hang by the delicate threads of a synthetic fiber?

Man's natural curiosity, perhaps, or some inner drive to satisfy a personal challenge. But deliberately to fling one's self from a high-flying perch thousands of feet above earth is certainly not for the faint of heart. And to do it continuously and safely demands nerve, skill, and self-discipline. There is nothing quite like the thrilling sensation of stepping into space, falling free for a mile or more, then completing the adventure silently and gently under an open canopy.

As any active jumper will say, "Skydiving is just plain fun—period!"

Sport parachutists find the momentary freedom in the air, the elation of being strictly and inexorably "on their own" during long, lonely descents, a pleasantly stimulating diversion from the monotony of daily routine. Oddly, skydiving is both relaxing and invigorating.

Much has been done to erase the popular image of the parachute jumper as a bold, brash, reckless daredevil. In the days of the flying circus, the jumper was a stuntman. No air show could succeed without him. However, a closely coordinated, carefully supervised national program has made parachuting an accepted, though dangerous, sport. Nevertheless, the enthusiasts who jump as a hobby are still a breed apart.

With few exceptions, "fun jumpers" are not flying beatniks or aerial hot-rodders. They hail from all walks of life, and include doctors, lawyers, bankers, students, servicemen, housewives, and secretaries. Some hold pilot licenses; others had never flown in an airplane until they went up for their first jump. Most have a strong desire for adventure or a burning ambition to excel.

Stephen Reyn White, of Wichita, Kansas, traded a fancy imported motorcycle for his first parachute rig. Three years after his first jump, young White was spending all his spare time running his Air Capital Para Center while completing courses in liberal arts and anthropology at Wichita State University.

The best advice to the beginner comes from Tiny Broadwick, who made her first jump from a hot-air balloon in 1908:

> Three main factors affect parachute landings—the jumper's rate of descent, drift speed over the ground, and oscillation. To land standing up requires considerable practice. (*Henry M. Dittmer*)

"I think skydiving is a wonderful sport, but those planning to try it should first learn all about parachutes before they go up. They must make sure everything about that first jump is a complete success."

Probably the most formidable barrier to a broader acceptance of parachuting as a popular sport is the fear most people have of falling. Even the most experienced parachutists will admit to some apprehension.

"Anyone who says he has never been afraid before a jump is joking," said Miss Urte Kaye after completing her 139th leap. "Every time I go up I have butterflies."

Modern sport clubs have good training programs to instill confidence, and competent jumpmasters are assigned to accompany students. The novice who appears overly nervous or feels sick is usually ordered to remain in the plane and postpone the jump until later. Sometimes pride compels a man to jump under almost any circumstances. That can be dangerous.

Back in 1935 Captain Harry G. Armstrong, then director of the Physiological Research Laboratory, Materiel Division of the United States Army Air Corps, undertook a series of test jumps to study the effects of free fall on the human body. Reporting his findings in the *Journal of the American Medical Association*, he concluded:

1. The mental reactions are normal, except as influenced by fear, excitement or other factors not attributable to the fall.

2. There is produced only one abnormal physical sensation and this consists of a very gentle, evenly distributed, generalized, superficial pressure on the downward surface of the body.
3. There is an apparent diminution of hearing acuity from an undetermined cause.
4. Position in space and motion through space are recognized solely by vision.
5. Depth perception acuity is such that a speed of approximately 100 feet per second at a distance of 1,900 feet from an object is required to recognize motion toward that object.
6. Delayed parachute jumps are an entirely practical means of avoiding certain hazardous aerial situations.

Captain Armstrong, who had never parachuted before, revealed a high state of anxiety in the moments leading up to the jump. He leaped from an open-cockpit Army biplane flying 119 miles an hour at 2,200 feet. The doctor dropped free 1,200 feet in a slow, tumbling fall, his body making a complete revolution every two seconds. He then opened his chute and descended normally.

No one can properly learn how to parachute jump *safely* by reading a book. Therefore, our objective is to acquaint the beginner with some of the most important things he should know before he pursues this fascinating space-age hobby.

Most sport parachutists, whether novice or veteran, belong to the Parachute Club of America. PCA membership is open to anyone, at least sixteen years of age, who is interested in parachuting. At this writing dues are $9.50 a year, which includes the cost of credentials, lapel emblem, a decal, the monthly PCA magazine *Parachutist*, and personal-liability insurance.

The insurance protects members from liability to persons and property injured or damaged as a result of a sport or exhibition jump. Public-liability coverage ranges from $5,000 for bodily injury to each person to $10,000 for each accident. The policy also includes $5,000 property damage to others.

Though optional, members are encouraged to join the National Aeronautic Association of which PCA is a non-profit division. NAA membership costs $5 a year, including credentials, lapel wings, the monthly magazine *National Aeronautics*, and $2,500 travel accident insurance and $250 medical-expense injury insurance good for travel accidents other than parachuting. A major goal of NAA is to stage an international Olympics of the Air for parachuting, soaring, ballooning, aerobatic flying, and model airplanes.

Not long after it was founded, PCA drew up a set of Basic Safety Regulations based upon recommendations of the nation's top jumpers. To keep pace with the sport's growth, these rules undergo continuous review and improvement. Their purpose is effectively to maintain and

develop the best possible standards of safety for encouraging and conducting organized parachuting as a
popular recreational activity.

Until recently the Federal government did little to
control parachuting, always holding the pilot responsible
for any object dropped from his plane—including people.
The old Civil Aeronautics Administration, now FAA,
established, but seldom enforced, parachuting minimums
for opening altitudes and surface wind velocities. Later,
after a series of air-show accidents, CAA banned delayed
jumping, but not for long.

Finally, FAA, concerned over the sport's mushroom-
ing growth and some of the old surplus equipment being
used, drafted new regulations governing all non-emergency parachute jumping. The new rules are intended
to help safeguard both public and parachutists, as well as
to minimize the obvious dangers to aircraft operating in
the navigable airspace.

Sport parachuting thrives in all fifty states. Some
states permit it under applicable Federal law; others
charge their aeronautics commissions with regulating
such activity. As a sport, skydiving is condoned, en-
dorsed, or condemned, depending on where you live.

Massachusetts, host for the sixth world championships,
in 1960 created a state parachuting board. California
leads all other states in number of active PCA members,
and probably has the most restrictions. Written with
PCA assistance, they are more stringent than those of the

FAA. New York, which once prohibited jumping if advertised as public entertainment, now allows it under state police jurisdiction.

Most states that feel a need for additional regulation use PCA's safety doctrine as a guide. New Jersey is the latest to pattern its controls after PCA rules. Vermont issues jumping permits to qualified PCA members only, but forbids use of state airports as permanent drop zones. Illinois and Idaho tolerate the sport, though very reluctantly.

In Texas, parachuting comes under the state's commission on higher education. An act passed in 1959 authorizes Texas colleges and universities to sponsor parachute clubs, provided they adhere to PCA safety criteria.

Throughout the country intercollegiate jumping is rivaling long-established competitive athletic programs. Annual meets to determine the best college parachutists have attracted as many as 60 contestants from 20 schools. Harvard University, one of the sport's top proponents, fields at least two teams and enjoys a string of victories in formal competition.

In about every large population center across the land there is weekend parachuting within a few minutes' drive. In less dense areas it is even nearer. The local Federal Aviation Agency office or airport operator is the best source for information on where to find skydiving in a particular region.

Skydiving enthusiasts band together in small groups

or clubs for operational, economic, and fraternal reasons. The experienced jumpers train the beginners, and all share in purchasing equipment and in renting or buying aircraft. Organized groups usually have drop zones away from busy airports to avoid traffic problems.

There are organized clubs in every state and in every principal city—more than 350 at last count. About 30 per cent are affiliated with PCA. Some are limited to civilian members, others to military, and still other clubs are composed of both. American sport jumpers overseas have clubs in Europe, Asia, and the Far East. Parachuting is also big in Panama and in Canada.

Typical of the more active groups, the California Parachute Club based at Livermore, and a PCA affiliate, was formed in 1956 to "encourage, promote and further develop amateur parachuting and skydiving." New members, if novices, pay $59 the first year, which includes a $30 initiation fee, annual dues of $15, a logbook, $2.50 handbook, and PCA membership costing $9.50. License-holding PCA members are charged only $5 initiation, plus yearly dues of $15.

Qualified club instructors conduct training classes for new members who are not experienced parachutists. The instruction embraces landing techniques, parachute packing, aircraft exiting, reserve-chute operation, emergency procedures and so forth.

The club is open to men and women over eighteen years of age. Candidates under twenty-one must have a signed release from their parents or guardian. All prospective members must pass a rigid physical examination, sign a waiver releasing the club from any liability, and join PCA. If in training it becomes apparent that a student cannot master the required skills, the club expels him.

Parachute equipment is available to members at a rental rate of $3 per jump, but each person must provide his or her own boots, coveralls, goggles, helmet, and gloves. In addition, the aircraft fare per jump runs from $3.50 up, depending on the altitude.

The expense of learning to leap will vary from club to club, largely because of local monthly or yearly dues. Price of personal gear, excluding parachute equipment, averages around $35 everywhere. For the true skydiving fan, new sport parachute outfits, main pack and reserve, are available for $350 or more. Modified surplus military jump sets approved by FAA are on the market for $100 up—but it's best to inspect such equipment thoroughly before buying.

It might seem an expensive indulgence, yet the costs of participating in sport parachuting are quite nominal when compared with scuba diving, drag racing, or even skeet shooting.

Out in Olathe, Kansas, site of the 1962 national parachuting championships, the Ka-Mo Sport Jumpers, Inc., operate strictly by the PCA book. Organized in 1959 with nine charter members, Ka-Mo now has about 50 regular skydivers from the metropolitan Kansas City, Missouri, area. Dues are $10 a month, a little higher than average, but the club operates its own Cessna, and charges only $1 per jump up to 7,000 feet.

As a result of the steadily increasing public interest in the sport, nearly two dozen commercial parachute centers have opened in the United States within the past five years. These enterprises are operated in a fashion similar to ski centers, some even offering accommodations and other resort facilities.

One of the first, the Orange Sport Parachuting Center founded in 1959, nestles in the rolling green hills of north-central Massachusetts, not far from the New Hampshire line. On any clear day with light winds, the sky above Orange is dotted with the blossoms of brightly colored parachutes. And on weekends a commodious spectator area is crowded with motorists from as far away as New York and Philadelphia.

The "first jump" course at Orange takes only three hours and costs $30, which includes all ground training, the airplane and equipment rental. Licensed instructors take great pains to ensure the fledgling's readiness for that first big step, yet the beginner course is limited to the essential fundamentals needed for a completely safe parachute descent.

PCA regulations require each student parachutist to make a minimum of five supervised jumps using a static line—a nylon strap hooked to the airplane which automatically releases the main chute after a short drop of less than 12 feet. After the first leap, static-line jumps cost about $5 each.

Paratroopers of the United States Army
101st Airborne Division trail static lines in
fast exit from Lockheed C-130 turboprop
carrier which can deliver 68 combat-ready
fighting men. (*Joe M. Gonzales*)

When the novice advances to free fall, he can take a delayed-jumping course at Orange for $15, plus the air-lift and equipment charges. And once he has his jump form down pat, he is ready for long delays—or skydiving. It starts with five-second free falls from about 3,000 feet, gradually increasing the exit altitude to 12,500 feet and delays lasting a full minute. After that, the sky's the limit!

For those desiring to develop free-fall skills, Orange and most other commercial centers offer lessons covering every phase of parachuting—spotting, stability, steering, tracking, turns, barrel rolls, spin control, instrument use, stable openings, and advanced canopy handling. Training in these skydiving techniques will range from $4 to $5 a lesson to the $8 or $10 price of special instruction in relative work—baton passing in midair between two or more free-falling jumpers.

In its first three seasons, the Orange center launched a total of nearly 11,000 jumpers. More than 1,600 were beginners. There were only 51 injuries, such as sprains, bruises, and fractures.

There are also commercial parachute centers in California, Texas, Ohio, New Jersey, Wisconsin, Kansas, Washington, Utah, and Arkansas. Enterprising enthusiasts in other states are at work planning similar operations even as this is written. Unfortunately, several of the centers are badly managed and may soon close their doors. Most operate well within the bounds of PCA and FAA precepts, however.

Sport parachuting is a far cry from professional exhibition jumping. In flying-circus days, chute jumps were described as "death-defying spectacles" for the morbidly curious. The only thing that really counted was executing a heart-stopping free fall guaranteed to give the crowd its money's worth.

Modern parachutists approach their calling scientifically. Instructors examine student performance with an analytical eye, recording every movement and action from the time the jumpmaster shouts "Go!" until the beginner lands and rolls up his parachute. Most clubs and centers also make it a practice to hold post-jump critiques.

The experienced parachutist has a good knowledge of aerodynamic principles relating to falling bodies. He can calculate pressures on various parts of the body during long delays and can measure the degree of stress on any component of his parachute equipment.

Equally important, the veteran skydiver can also compute with precise accuracy the rates of vertical descent, horizontal glide, turns and drifts. And he can tell you within a split second the time elapsed in free fall, and the exact distance of delay.

All man-carrying parachutes must meet certain FAA requirements for strength, operation, and maintenance. In addition, airplanes used to drop jumpers must be FAA-approved. Specified types are authorized for skydiving operations with one door removed. They include most Cessna, Piper, Aeronca, Stinson, and Taylorcraft single-engine aircraft, some Beechcraft twin-engine models, and several Howard and Noorduyn series.

Actually, almost any type of high-wing airplane, and many low-wing models, can be employed for parachuting. However, the craft should be capable of flying at relatively low speeds, say around 70 miles per hour or less, while holding its altitude and heading. Light cabin planes are ideally suited for jumping.

Under PCA regulations, all parachutists must open their packs at least 2,500 feet above the ground. Therefore, most static-line jumps are made from 2,600 feet, sometimes higher. No matter how high or low, however, a successful jump begins with the correct selection of the exit point.

Let's assume a student has successfully completed his three hours of ground training and now faces the big test —his first jump. As he climbs into the airplane, everything seems unreal. It's like a dream. He finds it almost impossible to believe that he is actually going up to jump out.

If the student is an average sort, he won't be able to think straight, swallow normally, or conceal his fright. That his instructor will fly with him as jumpmaster offers very little real comfort. Our student at this point would much rather be home in bed—or under it. His hands are clammy, his heart pounds, and his stomach feels queasy. Though nearly numb with fear, he tries desperately to remember all that he's been told.

The jumpmaster supervises parachuting operations.

It is his responsibility to select the course to fly, direct the pilot, and pick out the correct ground reference point over which the student will leave the airplane. This is called spotting.

At the jump altitude, in this instance 2,500 feet, the plane is flown into the wind and directly over a large X target in the drop zone (DZ) below. As the plane flies over the target, the jumpmaster drops a weighted cloth streamer to indicate wind-drift direction and speed. A streamer is about 20 feet long. With a small weight attached to one end, it will fall at approximately the same rate as an open parachute.

Based on where the streamer lands, in relation to the ground target, the jumpmaster then selects an exit point the same distance from the X but in the opposite direction.

The jumper usually leaves the aircraft in one of two ways—the poised exit used mainly from smaller, slower planes, or the door exit, which is best suited for larger, faster aircraft. Because our student will jump from a high-wing Cessna cabin monoplane, he will use the *poised* exit.

Now all is ready. The student has assumed his proper sitting position in the Cessna's open doorway; the jumpmaster has spotted the exit point; and the pilot has headed the plane back into the wind over the target. The jumpmaster makes a final static-line check to ensure that both ends are still secure.

Approaching the exit point, the pilot throttles down

and holds the plane just above stalling speed to reduce wind blast. The student places his feet on the Cessna's step or wheel, pulls himself through the door, and grabs the wing strut. Over the spot, he braces on the strut and, at the jumpmaster's signal, thrusts his feet up toward the rear and pushes himself back and away from the airplane into what is termed a stable-fall position.

In the basic stable fall, a horizontal face-to-earth position, the body is arched, the legs are spread apart with knees slightly bent, and the arms are extended out with palms down and a small crook in the elbow.

As the student drops away from the airplane, he counts "one thousand, two thousand, three thousand . . ." and so forth. By "four thousand" his parachute should be open, for it takes one second to say each thousand at a normal speaking rate.

Because his is a static-line jump, the student's parachute begins opening automatically about a second after he leaves the airplane. He falls 10 or 12 feet; the static line stretches tight, pulls the pack pins, and releases the pilot chute.

Once the pilot chute clears the container and springs open, things happen fast. The pilot acts as a sea anchor and draws the main canopy and shroud lines from the pack. As the jumper continues to fall until his suspension lines are completely paid out, the top of the canopy traps air and starts to inflate. Next, the skirt bursts open with a *voom*, snapping the jumper upright.

From the time the static line unpacks the chute, the

whole opening sequence takes less than three seconds.

Unless the parachute is equipped with sleeve deployment, the opening shock will range from moderately severe to a head-jarring jolt. For as the inflating canopy swallows air, it builds up a tremendous force of resistance that almost instantaneously jerks the jumper from a high-speed fall to a very slow rate of descent. Yet no matter how badly it rattles his teeth, to our student the opening shock is the greatest feeling in the world.

Chances are that the beginner will shout his unbridled exuberance for all on earth to hear as he floats gently down under that big, beautiful nylon umbrella.

Suspended under a 28-foot canopy, the jumper usually sinks about 16 to 21 feet per second, often landing no harder than as if he had stepped from the top of a compact car. The degree of modification, of course, such as open gores and other air vents, will have some effect on glide speeds. Soviet competition chutes descend hot— about 30 feet per second.

The rate of descent is also affected by atmospheric density as well as by canopy diameter. Jumpers fall faster on hot days, when the air is thin, than they do on cold days, when the air is dense. A parachutist might be dropping unusually fast, then suddenly pass through a pocket of cooler, heavier air. This will induce a braking action, like dumping the flaps on an airplane.

After realizing that his chute *did* work, the excited student looks up and checks his lines and canopy. He also remembers that regardless of how much inherent stability has been built into a sport parachute canopy, there's always a certain amount of oscillation—a pendulum-like motion. Unless arrested in time, it could whip him into the ground with a bone-splintering crunch.

Inches from touchdown, Reyn White, of Wichita, Kansas, drives hard toward target center in accuracy jump as *fichet* Larry Adams, right, gets set to mark first contact point. (*Henry M. Dittmer*)

How to control oscillation by manipulating the canopy is a part of every basic parachuting course. One way is to pull or pump the two front risers, or lift webs, in the forward half of the arc, releasing them on the back swing. This is known as a two-riser slip. Another acceptable method is to pull one front and one diagonally-opposed rear lift web. Called a one-riser slip, it allows the jumper to work against both ends of the arc, dumping air on each side to neutralize the oscillation.

Finally our student nears the end of his first jump. He well recalls the emphasis placed by his instructor on PLF (parachute landing fall) techniques. There are several ways, but the main thing is to be fairly relaxed with legs slightly bent and moderately tense. A slight tension enables the muscular system to absorb the landing shock.

Facing his line of drift, the student contacts the ground, rotating his body as he falls over. This permits his buttocks to receive the major force of the impact. He even remembers to give a vigorous tug on the risers at the instant of touchdown to help cushion the blow.

It's all over. He did it. As he scrambles to his feet, takes off his harness, and rolls up his chute, a wonderful sense of conquest, impossible to achieve in any other way, suddenly engulfs him. He is enormously happy, proud, triumphant.

But the important thing he must always remember is that in parachuting, the learning never ceases. Every succeeding jump is a new experience, a new challenge. No two are ever alike.

ADVANCED SKYDIVING

5

SIR ISAAC NEWTON, THE NOTED ENGLISH ASTRONOMER, mathematician, and natural philosopher who lived from 1642 to 1727, formulated the laws of gravity. The story goes that a falling apple hit Sir Isaac on the head, suggesting to him that all particles of matter in the universe must exert an attraction on one another. In any case, Newton's discovery was one of the most important in the history of natural science.

How gravity relates to skydiving is obvious. The speed of a falling body increases at a uniform rate until it reaches a terminal velocity. If there were no air, everything from a tennis ball to a fire truck would fall at the same rate of speed—pulled down by the forces of gravity.

Yet any object moving through the earth's atmosphere creates friction. And eventually the gravitational pull and the friction will balance out. From then on, the object falls at a constant speed, or at terminal velocity.

A parachutist jumping from relatively low altitudes, assuming for the moment that there is no forward speed,

will drop about 16 feet the first second. He will continue
to accelerate until he reaches a terminal velocity of about
174 feet per second, or about 120 miles an hour. This
takes about 12 seconds of free fall.

However, atmospheric density diminishes with altitude; the higher in the sky, the thinner the air. Consequently, as forces of friction decrease, the jumper falls
proportionately faster. His terminal velocity would ex-
ceed 174 feet per second. But as the parachutist drops
into heavier air at the lower altitudes, friction increases,
slowing his fall to the normal rate.

Momentarily, the forward speed of an aircraft serving
as a jump platform will affect the rate of fall. For the
first few seconds, the parachutist travels in the same direction and very nearly at the same velocity as the airplane. That is why pilots bailing out of high-speed jets
must delay opening their parachutes. If a pilot ejects at
600 miles an hour, for example, and releases his chute
instantly, the resultant stresses can be fatal.

Another important factor which influences the jumper's vertical speed is the position of his body in free fall.
If he dives straight down, his body offers less than two
square feet of air resistance. But by falling flat with arms
and legs spread apart as in the "basic stable position," he
has about ten square feet of body surface to resist the air.
A tumbling body also falls slower than one diving
straight.

Gravitational pull, the air pressure against the downward side of his body, and the airflow around him are the

three main forces that act upon a parachutist in free fall.

An equal balance of these three forces will produce stabilization. Yet any change in the attitude of the jumper's body while in a stable free fall will upset the balance. Any slight movement of an arm, leg, hand, or foot will abruptly change body position, and to some extent his falling speed and direction. This is how sky-divers achieve different maneuvers during delayed drops.

There are several basic "stable" positions used in sky-diving, such as high spread, frog, turn, and delta, to list a few. Each has moderate and extreme variations for free-fall aerobatics—loops, rolls, turns, somersaults, glides, and the precision maneuvering required in ad-vanced relative work.

Already described is the "stable-fall" or "stable-spread" position, the most popular and basic of all. It is the attitude most jumpers assume as they leave the air-craft, whether by a poised or door exit. For a door exit, the parachutist stands erect, steps into space in the stable-fall position, and aligns himself with the plane's flight path. Another way is to dive out, toward the rear of the ship, immediately assuming a delta spread in which the arms are drawn back at angles of 30 or 45 degrees.

The delta position is perhaps the most exciting in that the jumper not only travels at maximum velocity but also falls in a head-down attitude.

In the true delta position the parachutist tries to keep his body as straight as possible. He holds the arms straight, drawn in along the sides and then pushed back,

Rod Pack performs a "back loop" for photographer Jim Lizzio's helmet-mounted camera.

The maneuver looks
deceptively easy,
but it demands a great
deal of practice.

rolling the shoulders forward. His legs are straight and spread slightly with the toes pointed. A delta expert can attain speeds of more than 200 miles an hour in long delays.

Tracking is accomplished effectively only by the sky-diver proficient in maintaining complete control over both the vertical and horizontal axes of his body.

Similar in appearance to the delta position, the jumper in a maximum-track attitude, if properly executed under ideal conditions, can travel one foot horizontally for every foot and a half of vertical fall. Instead of arching the back as in other positions, the jumper inclines his body at a slight angle, with his head lower than the feet. Arms are kept close to the sides with palms down, fingers together and hands cupped. Legs are also held straight as if standing on the toes at attention.

Any lateral line of flight is known as tracking or glid-ing. It is essential to relative work, and demands a great deal of skill. In tracking attitude most skydivers reach an average speed of around 180 miles per hour.

Most sport parachuting is done below 15,000 feet. Some 80 per cent of all premeditated jumps are within an altitude range of 2,500 to 8,000 feet above ground. Yet many jumps are made at heights above 20,000 feet, even over 30,000 feet, with the aid of small, portable oxygen equipment.

Men developing and testing parachutes more than forty years ago did so within the confines of low-performance aircraft, most of which were unable to fly very high. Knowing little about the upper atmosphere, they questioned a parachute's ability to function properly at high altitudes. As a result, the first high-altitude jumps were to test parachute operation.

Sergeant Ralph Bottriel of the Army parachute research team at McCook Field conducted the first live experiment. He argued that if the air four or five miles up could support the wings of an airplane, it could also inflate a parachute canopy and support the weight of a man suspended beneath.

On June 28, 1921, the courageous Bottriel set out to prove his point, ignoring a warning that if the canopy did deploy at 20,000 feet, the opening shock in such thin air would tear it to shreds. Climbing into the rear seat of a LePere biplane, he flew up to 20,500 feet and prepared to bail out.

Standing on the seat, Bottriel attempted to signal the pilot, and inadvertently snagged his ripcord. The pack spilled, cracked open, and jerked the terrified sergeant out of the cockpit with an explosive force that drove his body through the tail, ripping away part of the fin and rudder. Stunned, his left arm smashed by the impact, Bottriel by some miracle finally cleared the airplane and descended under his open parachute.

Though weak from shock, lack of oxygen, and loss of blood, the plucky sergeant managed to wrap a shroud line around his shattered arm for a perfect tourniquet.

Harold Osborne is shown with his main chute tangled in the tail of this Douglas O-25A in a 1931 training jump. He finally cut himself free to descend safely with his reserve. (*U.S. Air Force*)

Bottriel's feat marked the first scientific high-altitude parachute jump in aviation history. Then, three years later, in 1924, Captain A. W. Stevens of McCook Field's photographic section set a new record by jumping from a supercharged Martin bomber at 26,500 feet.

Probably the first scientifically planned free fall of any

significance was Arthur H. Starnes's record delay from
30,800 feet to 1,500 feet in 1941.

Starnes, an aerial stunt man who once teamed with
Roscoe Turner, started performing delayed drops in
1925. He soon perfected his free-fall technique to the
point where he could leap from 10,000 feet, delay his
opening to within several hundred feet of the ground,
then land in a predetermined area no bigger than a bed-
sheet. But his experiment in 1941 was without question
his greatest performance.

The jump was conceived and executed with the aid of
physiologists and medical doctors to prove that a properly equipped airman could survive long delays from
"substratospheric" altitudes without suffering any ill
effects.

Starnes carried nearly 100 pounds of extra equipment
to record his fall. In addition to his two parachutes, he
wore a heated flying suit with heated boots and gloves.
He had an oxygen bailout bottle with a mask. A radio
strapped around his waist transmitted his heartbeats. A
pneumograph measured his breathing. On his right hip
he fixed a movie camera to film the view.

The ex-barnstormer fell over five and a half miles before opening his parachute. Instruments revealed that his
rate of fall slowed from 150 to 13 miles an hour when the
chute blossomed. The opening shock was so terrific he
blacked out.

One objective of the big jump was to demonstrate the
practicability of long delays as a safe, sure method of

evading enemy-aircraft gunfire. With most of the world already at war, there were all too many cases of combat flyers escaping their crippled planes at high altitudes, only to become "shooting-gallery" targets as they descended under open parachutes.

But the main purpose of the jump was to gather data necessary for designing equipment that would ensure the safety of flight crews manning the high-performance aircraft of the future. It was a kind of prelude to later, more exhaustive, military research efforts, such as the United States Air Force's Project Excelsior.

Excelsior, a high-altitude survival program aimed at developing special equipment and techniques for airmen forced to abandon their aerospace craft, involved three of the most incredible parachute jumps in aviation annals—all made by Captain Joseph W. Kittinger, Jr., USAF. Jumps were made from 76,400 feet, 75,000 feet, and finally from 102,800 feet, the very edge of space.

On the third and last Excelsior leap, made in August, 1960, from an open balloon gondola, Captain Kittinger began his drop nearly 20 miles up, above 99 per cent of the earth's atmosphere. His free fall lasted more than four and a half minutes, during which he achieved, at the higher, rarefied levels, a vertical speed of 614 miles per hour. His main chute opened at 18,000 feet, ending a record-breaking delay of 84,800 feet.

For his historic jumps, Captain Kittinger used a multi-stage parachute developed by Francis Beaupre and other members of the Excelsior team. It is designed to deploy

Captain Joseph W. Kittinger, Jr., USAF, begins the highest altitude drop in history —102,800 feet— on August 16, 1960. An automatic camera attached to the balloon's gondola, which served as jump platform, recorded the start of his leap. (*U.S. Air Force*)

at great heights and stabilize in free fall the airman who leaps in the stratosphere.

The Beaupre chute is worn as a conventional parachute. When deployed at extremely high altitudes, the first stage opens to a diameter of six feet. This slows the jumper only slightly, but provides outstanding feet-first falling control, thus eliminating the danger of a deadly flat spin. At a preset altitude of 14,000 to 19,000 feet, an automatic timing device operated by an aneroid barometer releases the main canopy.

A modified Beaupre parachute is intended as standard equipment for the National Aeronautics and Space Administration's two-man Gemini spacecraft.

Soviet Russia refuses to acknowledge Kittinger's long leap as a bona-fide free fall because the United States Air Force officer used a stabilizing chute. Russia claims that Major Yvegeny N. Andreyev, of the Soviet Air Force, set a new world's record on November 1, 1962, when he jumped from 83,502 feet, without any stabilizing device, and fell free for 79,560 feet before opening his parachute.

Major Andreyev, accompanied by Colonel Peter I. Dolgov, who was scheduled to make a regular jump, went aloft in a hermetically sealed balloon gondola. After the major leaped on his free fall, Colonel Dolgov stepped out at 93,968 feet, opened his chute immediately, and was killed during the descent.

The Soviet authorities have never divulged the exact cause of Dolgov's death. Both he and Major Andreyev were active in testing high-speed aircraft escape systems as well as parachute ejection devices for the series of Vostok manned spaceships. Dolgov was one of Russia's best known jumpers, and the holder of eight Soviet and world parachute records.

Although the Soviets claimed that Andreyev's jump disproved the theory that a stabilizing chute was essential in very long free falls, they later admitted that the major had gone into several dangerous spins during his 15-mile drop.

Andreyev reportedly fell for 15,000 to 20,000 feet flat on his back to keep the transparent visor on his heated helmet from frosting. His top speed was 558 miles an hour. As he entered the denser layers of atmosphere, Andreyev turned face downward and assumed the sky-diver's conventional stable-spread position. He also changed to a maximum-track attitude, forming a 40-degree angle of descent to avoid landing in the Volga River.

At an altitude of five or six miles, his speed had slowed to about 145 miles an hour. At about 4,920 feet Major Andreyev received an automatic signal. He then opened his parachute manually at 3,152 feet.

According to the Fédération Aéronautique Internationale, which governs all official aviation records and competitions, the previous world mark for a delayed opening jump was established by a Soviet sport parachutist. FAI records show that on August 20, 1961, skydiver Nikolai Nikitin jumped from 50,469 feet and fell free for 46,965 feet at Engels Airport near Saratov, Russia.

Old theories that a free fall of 100 feet or more produced unconsciousness and even death were exploded in the early 1920's, by chance at first, then by intentional delayed jump tests. Soon exhibition jumpers were regularly performing spectacular delays lasting thousands of feet.

Actually, there is no sensation of falling in a long delay, or of sinking. The parachutist doesn't lose his breath or even his ability to see and think clearly. In fact, it's more like floating on an ocean of air.

Depending upon the exit altitude and body position, a jumper in free fall will drop 120 miles an hour or more. But even at that velocity his only impression of speed is a terrific blast of wind tearing at his clothing. In a stable-spread attitude, he feels a gentle pressure on the downward surfaces of his arms, legs and body. The nearest possible similar earthly experience is that of being lowered slowly into a bed of softest down.

Leaving the airplane several thousands of feet up, a jumper can rapidly accelerate to a velocity of 200 miles an hour or more by holding his body vertical—the delta. By lying flat with arms and legs extended as in the stable-spread position, he lounges along at a mere 120 miles per hour.

To make horizontal headway, the parachutist positions his body so that it resembles somewhat the cross section of an airplane wing, his maximum-tracking attitude. By dropping an extended arm to his side, he turns in that direction. Pulling that arm into his chest, coupled with a twisting body motion, he'll go into a barrel roll. Forward with the arms, back with the head, up to the chest with the knees—a graceful backward loop. And by snapping into a jackknife position, a forward loop.

It sounds simple enough, but it requires intense training and practice. And it must be done fast! If the jumper begins his free fall at 13,500 feet, the ground is less than 80 seconds away, unless part of the trip is covered by parachute.

While plunging through space, the skydiver has a kaleidoscopic view of the sweeping panorama below him.

Navy photographer Donald "Chip" Maury is snapped at 7,000 feet by a fellow Chuting Star, Edward Kruse. Notice the 35-mm. Nikon strapped on Maury's wrist. (*U.S. Navy*)

Once he trains his eye, he can pick out features—buildings, moving vehicles, landmarks. His greatest danger is not that he'll spin into unconsciousness but that he will get carried away by the fun of it all.

Losing track of altitude can lead to disaster. That's why most experienced jumpers now mount both stop watches and altimeters on top of their reserve chutes. They check one instrument against the other as double insurance. French parachutists have buzzers that sound inside their helmets at the right moment, the way a kitchen timer goes off when the roast is done.

Misjudging altitude and purposely delaying the opening beyond safe margins are the causes of most fatal accidents today. This is especially true in relative work, where it is easy to become deeply absorbed in attempting baton passes.

Another ugly hazard is target fixation, a deadly phenomenon known to fighter pilots. This is a sort of self-hypnosis induced by excessive concentration on a ground or air target. Pilots have actually flown directly into their targets, without any apparent attempt to pull up or away, undoubtedly driven by an overwhelming desire to achieve a good gunnery score.

The sport parachutist faces similar dangers. Or he allows himself to become so enraptured by the stimulating experience of free fall that he completely forgets the passage of time. When he finally pulls his ripcord, it may be too late.

Out of 45 parachuting fatalities reported to PCA during the years 1958 through 1962, failure to pull either ripcord accounted for 18. Four other deaths were attributed to late openings. These statistics alone present an impressive case for using a reserve chute equipped with a device that will automatically activate it at a preset altitude of about 1,000 feet.

Many jumpers practice verbal counting in delays up to eight seconds. For longer free falls, the careful parachutist will rely on his instruments—both altimeter and stop watch.

As the jumper accumulates experience, the involuntary gyrations of his early leaps become well planned, carefully coordinated, magnificently executed aerobatic maneuvers. Loops, rolls, and fast turns are no longer uncontrolled tumbling as in a disorderly fall. They are performed intentionally and with a graceful, exacting precision.

Certainly the most exciting—if not the most dangerous —phase of skydiving is relative work with one or more partners. Writing in *Canadian Parachutist*, Daryl Henry, Canada's top-ranking skydiver who placed sixth in the 1962 world championships, put it this way:

"Sharing the free space playground with another parachutist opens a unique realm of experience comparable to nothing known to man. It is unlimited joy, and complicated with danger. Whereas once one's safety was under his own private control it must now come under another's jurisdiction also. And you suddenly become responsible for his life as well as your own."

Actually, there have been few serious accidents in multiple jumps. One of the most tragic occurred in September, 1962, when two skydivers collided in the air over San Jose, California. James Nickolson and Paul Baitx had both leaped from a plane at 7,200 feet. A few seconds later Baitx pulled his ripcord. Witnesses reported that Nicholson plunged through the open canopy before his own opened. Baitx was killed, his fall only partially broken by his collapsing chute.

Relative work demands the utmost skill, nerve, and discipline. It requires delays of at least 30 seconds, and a highly developed ability to control precisely—within physical limitations, of course—vertical speed and direction during free fall.

The pinnacle of the sport is the baton pass. To accomplish the feat, two or more jumpers, one carrying a staff, leap within short intervals of each other, then glide together, exchange the baton, separate, and open their parachutes. As accurate communication between jumpers during free fall is virtually impossible, the first and most important prerequisite of successful baton passing is thorough planning.

Naturally, the ever present risk of a midair collision with your fellow parachutist constitutes the greatest hazard. Should two jumpers roar across each other's path at express-train speeds, the chances of their survival are very poor.

To plan a baton pass properly, the jumper must first select a compatible partner, one whose physique, weight, and proficiency are basically the same as his. Terminal velocities will not only vary in different body positions but also among different sizes of parachutists as well. This might be imperceptible in single fall, yet the degree of variance, regardless of how small, will have a tremendous effect on successful relative work.

Three factors affect terminal velocity: frontal body area, body weight or bulk, and surface friction, in that order. In the stable-spread position, for example, a man six feet two inches tall and weighing 190 pounds would fall slower than a man of equal weight but shorter in stature.

Also essential to planning are the individual functions in the attempted baton pass, the order of exit, who will carry the staff first, the respective trajectories after leaving the jump plane, alternatives, visual signals, the altitudes for terminating the attempt, the separation, and the safe opening.

Maneuvering in free fall to swap something the size of a hatchet handle takes expert body control, absolute concentration, and perfect timing. Too many tries will eat up hundreds of feet of precious altitude.

Baton passing is believed to have originated in France about 1950. Not until June, 1958, did Lyle Hoffman and Jim Pearson make the first recorded baton pass in North America. They turned the trick in the first 30 seconds of a 60-second delay from 12,000 feet over Van-

Marvin Steele, right, a 220-pounder, and Anne Batterson, who weighs 102 pounds, exit from a Cessna Skylane, then "track in" to pass a baton

r this series of
hotographs taken by
m Lizzio, one of
e sport's leading
xydiving photographers.
the last picture
e jumpers are sepa-
ting to unpack.

couver, British Columbia, while trying out for the United States parachute team.

One month later, in July, 1958, Charles Hillard and Steve Snyder, two students from Georgia Institute of Technology, completed the first known pass in the United States. They jumped from a USAF C-123 at 8,500 feet over Fort Bragg, North Carolina. Charlie Hillard is now one of the nation's top aerobatic exhibition pilots; Snyder operates a commercial parachute service.

Today baton passing is considered little more than another milestone in every sport parachutist's career. Multiple passes between experienced skydivers are fairly common—as many as five separate exchanges have been made in a single jump. It is still a very risky business, however.

Just as important as the ability to maneuver in free fall, if not more so, is the ability to manipulate an open parachute. Once the fledgling parachutist tries a few jumps, he will learn how to control his descent and drift direction with increasing accuracy. When conditions are favorable, he'll also find it possible to land standing up, though novices shouldn't try this until they become reasonably adept at canopy handling.

Space-age version of old horse-and-rider game is played by four members of the Army Golden Knights parachute team after a mass jump two miles up over the drop zone. (*Joe M. Gonzales*)

Every jumper must also be prepared for certain un-predictable eventualities. If a descending parachutist dis-covers that a tree landing is unavoidable, probably be-cause of a sudden surge in the wind velocities at lower levels, he simply crosses his legs and folds both arms in front of his face and throat.

Under no circumstances should the jumper attempt to grab a branch in the hope of breaking his fall. And if he hangs up in a tree higher than he can safely drop, he merely opens his reserve parachute, sheds his harness, and slides down the reserve suspension lines and canopy. Smokejumpers of the United States Forest Service have this technique down pat.

Landing in water is much the same as landing in a high wind. The jumper settles back in his harness, the seat webbing tucked well under his buttocks. As he nears the surface, he unsnaps leg straps first, then the chest strap. At the instant he strikes the water or ground, he raises his arms over his head, arches his back, and slides com-pletely out of the harness assembly.

Most modern parachutes have quick-release devices that connect the lift webs to the harness at the jumper's shoulders. The two fasteners are easily unsnapped at their attachment points, swiftly separating the jumper from his canopy.

The only way to become proficient in sport parachut-ing is by doing it, first under the watchful eye of a quali-fied instructor, later through practical experience. A man can absorb a lot of theory from a book, but it is no substitute for the real thing.

An addicted parachutist devoutly believes there is no limit to the physical and spiritual benefits he will derive by repeatedly hurling himself into space. It embraces the challenge of competition, the exaltation of soaring through the air, and the utter self-reliance a man is bound to feel when he has the choice of life or death at his fingertips.

No matter what the attraction, almost everyone who experiences free fall goes back for seconds.

HOW SAFE?

6

High in the clear blue sky overhead, a small light plane bores into the wind, its forward speed slowing as the pilot throttles back. Suddenly beneath the craft a speck appears, seemingly suspended in air at first. Then it falls, now a doll-like shape with arms outstretched and legs apart. Down the figure comes, faster and faster as it hurtles toward earth at a dizzy pace.

Seconds tick away. The crowd is silent, waiting breathlessly for a wisp of white to trail behind the plummeting body, unfurl, and billow open with a muffled snapping noise, like shaking a wet sheet. But the canopy never blossoms; nothing halts the mad, spine-chilling drop. A half-mile distant, young Clarence Gretencourt, with 20 successful military and sport jumps to his credit, plunges to the ground at 120 miles an hour.

This was the tragic scene on Sunday, July 21, 1963, at Great Bend, Kansas, where members of a Topeka sky-diving club were making delayed parachute jumps to help publicize a four-day rodeo. Gretencourt's body fell in an alfalfa field, some 850 yards from his target site east of the old Sante Fe Trail rodeo grounds.

The unlucky jumper died of multiple fractures, including a broken neck. He had leaped from 3,600 feet. Those who watched his fatal drop through binoculars saw no movement for the ripcord until it was too late. But to Ross Ailslieger, area safety officer for the Parachute Club of America, Gretencourt's death was no accident—"It was downright murder!"

Ailslieger reportedly told Federal Aviation Agency investigators and the press that earlier he had warned the Topeka skydivers against using their illegally modified equipment which, in his opinion, would never pass a government inspection. As a result, FAA district safety representatives prohibited the group from making a scheduled exhibition jump the following Sunday at the National Jalopy Championship races in nearby Hutchinson.

Federal concern over the growing number of people who are falling out of the sky attracted widespread attention in July, 1961, when FAA Administrator Najeeb E. Halaby went up for a bird's-eye look. After successfully completing his first premeditated parachute jump, Halaby observed:

"This can be a fine thing—an important and certainly an exhilarating new facet of national sport—or it can be a dangerous thing. Sport parachuting has enjoyed a tremendous increase in popularity during the past five years and new rules are necessary to assure that future growth occurs under proper conditions."

FAA's new rules came in the form of Federal Aviation Regulation Part 105, effective February 26, 1963, which makes parachutists, as well as pilots, responsible for the safe conduct of non-emergency jumps. Previously, only the aircraft pilot who dropped the jumper had this responsibility.

Part 105 prohibits sport or exhibition jumps over congested areas and open-air assemblies except as authorized by FAA. It also specifies that parachuting at airports with FAA control towers will first require tower approval. Jumping in other controlled airspace, such as the Federal airways, must be cleared through the appropriate air-traffic-control facility. The rules prescribe visibility standards, prohibit jumps through clouds, and require adequate lighting for night drops.

Under the new rules FAA extends the time limit for repacking main parachutes from 60 to 120 days, though it does not grant a similar extension to reserve chutes. While the person making the jump may pack his own main parachute, only FAA certificated riggers are allowed to pack reserves. Furthermore, only licensed senior or master parachute riggers may perform repairs, maintenance, or alterations on parachute equipment.

On the whole, FAR Part 105 rules governing sport parachuting are far less restrictive than the Parachute Club of America's own safety regulations. Many parachutists feel more stringent Federal standards are needed to help protect jumpers from breaking their necks.

FAA recognizes the fine contribution PCA is making

toward safety. As the predominant force in United States sport parachuting, PCA's program of self-regulation and policing has done more to develop safe practices in organized parachuting than any other factor. What worries both FAA and PCA most, however, are the cold, hard statistics showing little or no improvement in sport parachuting accident trends.

Early in 1963 PCA reported that the annual ratio of about one fatality for every 900 active jumpers has remained constant since 1958. This means that while the number of participants and jumps continued to increase each year for five years, so did the number of fatal accidents, and in direct proportion.

(Computed in the same way, motoring is still between two and three times safer. In 1963 there was one motor-vehicle fatality for every 2,300 licensed drivers in the United States.)

FAA has stated that PCA does a good job of keeping its own house in order. The club's adoption of common-sense rules has so far proved tremendously effective. But unless the death, injury, and complaint rates decline, FAA will write and enforce new punitive regulations, possibly even making it necessary for parachutists to obtain FAA jumping licenses.

"We believe that those participating in the sport can do much to chart the future by maintaining an acceptable accident level and properly respecting the public interest of others, both on the surface and as joint airspace users," says James F. Rudolph, chief of the operations division of FAA's flight standards service. "Sensationalism, fool-hardy operations, poor equipment, improper or no train-ing and lack of self-restraint are but a few typical ex-amples that do a disservice to the sport."

One such case occurred in western Illinois. Members of a local parachute club jumped at the scene of an air-plane accident, causing considerable damage to farm crops in the surrounding area. And in California jumpers have been known to break power lines and even land in the Rose Bowl during football games.

In various sections of the country there has been a tendency on the part of the police of major congested areas to outlaw the sport completely. Unfortunately, the irresponsible actions of a few clowns give the sport a black eye. The great majority of sport parachutists to-day are sensible, conscientious citizens of good character and integrity.

Rudolph also told the writer that there appears to be some misunderstanding with respect to the use of surplus military parachutes and modifications in general.

Better to qualify personnel charged with approving parachutes for sport jumping, FAA now sends selected field inspectors to the United States Forest Service smokejumper center at Missoula, Montana. There the inspectors, whose chief task is to certify the airworthi-ness of all flying machines based in their respective dis-tricts, become thoroughly indoctrinated in parachute design, construction, maintenance, and packing.

PCA investigates every serious sport-parachuting accident in the United States. Its findings are generally conclusive, and in almost every instance point to human frailty of some kind.

Parachuting has been vagariously described as "carefully controlled violence." True, men have tamed their unruly bundles of cloth, lines, and links through years of trial and error. Yet the parachute is a device quite capable of hurting, maiming, or killing the ill-suited user. For want of a better term, parachuting might be classed as a "contact" sport.

Competently surpervised training, strict compliance with all safety practices, and approved jumping procedures are vitally essential to longevity. As long as the parachutist plays the game according to all the rules and uses good equipment, he'll find skydiving a safe and richly rewarding hobby.

There are certain inherent hazards, but impeccable parachutes and jumping habits have eliminated many of the old dangers.

While rare in relation to the enormous number of uneventful jumps each year, parachute malfunctions can and do happen. Any improper functioning of the parachute while in use is called a "malfunction." There are two general types: a partial failure which reduces the rate of descent, and the complete failure which could be fatal. Yet for just about every adverse condition, there is a corrective action.

Partial malfunctions result when a shroud line ends up over the top of the canopy during the opening process.

Jack Huber, an old-timer who made hundreds of jumps, lands safely after having trouble with his main chute. He was killed in 1951. (*Bob McComb*)

The misplaced line squeezes the inflated canopy into the shape of a huge brassiere. Jumpers call this having a Mae West. Technically it is a partial inversion. Occasionally, more than one shroud line flips over the canopy, dividing the parachute's diameter to a fraction of its normal area. Often one or more lines can be cleared by working them down over the edge of the canopy.

A complete failure is just what the term implies. The canopy, upon release from its pack, fails to inflate at all. Yet as it "dishrags" above the falling jumper like a streaming ribbon, it creates a certain amount of drag. This is known as a streamer. The parachutist in this predicament falls feet first, in a good position to open his reserve pack.

Miss Lois Ann Frotten, now Mrs. John E. Burke, knows precisely what it's like to have a streamer. And undoubtedly she is one of the luckiest girls alive today, for several reasons.

On July 18, 1962, Miss Frotten and her fiancé gave each other an engagement present of sorts by agreeing to make their first parachute jump together, near Brewster, Massachusetts. Leaping from 2,500 feet, Burke landed safely. Lois Ann followed. She exited properly, and a static line attached to the plane opened her pack, but the chute streamed. Making no move to release her reserve, she hit a lake feet first, plunged 20 feet to the bottom and into soft mud.

She escaped with only two small vertebrae fractures and a cut nose. She and Burke were married on November 11, 1962. Before their wedding vows, the couple took another vow—never to skydive again.

Not so lucky was Dianne Elaine Tange, twenty, of San Gabriel, California, killed October 7, 1962, on her first jump. Miss Tange leaped from 2,600 feet. Her parachute also streamed out behind her but failed to open. In a futile attempt to save her, ex-Army paratrooper James Francel dived out of the same plane, hoping to overtake the girl and shout instructions to her. Francel finally pulled his own ripcord, landing safely moments after Miss Tange smashed into the ground at express-train speed.

Another problem that occurs infrequently results when a jumper tumbles through his lines or lift webs during the parachute-opening sequence. This may produce a slight twist at the bottom of his suspension lines, and nothing more. Or the canopy might turn completely inside out. In either case, the rate of sink is usually normal. Once in a while, however, this type of problem becomes compounded.

Louie Lujano of the Sierra View Skydivers had demonstrated outstanding form in free fall, but seemed to be experiencing some difficulty with terminal velocity ripcord pulls. Two weeks before his fatal leap at Fresno, California, on June 3, 1962, Louie had his first serious malfunction when the canopy sleeve caught between his legs. He deployed his reserve; then his main chute opened and Lujano rode both canopies down.

As a result of this incident, Louie Lujano determined

to perfect his pull in a series of jumps from 4,500 feet, instead of 6,500 feet where he had been starting his delays. He tried one, and everything worked fine.

He took off for his next jump and made a beautiful, poised exit from a Stinson V-77 flying at 4,500 feet. He held an extreme arch in a spread-eagle position and fell completely stable for 15 seconds, the planned duration of his free fall.

According to PCA's accident report, when Lujano went for his ripcord, he bent forward and tumbled violently as he pulled. The parachute came up between his legs while he turned over. Ground observers also noted that the jumper received a severe opening shock. After the canopy inflated, a bad malfunction was obvious. It appeared to be a complex "Mae West" involving several shroud lines over the canopy top and between Lujano's legs.

Lonie immediately activated his reserve chute, opening the pack and grabbing an armful of nylon material which he threw straight up, instead of out from his chest. Consequently, the reserve canopy became entangled in the main parachute's suspension lines. The partially inflating reserve also forced pressure on the lines over the top of his main canopy, further collapsing it.

The doomed jumper fell in a fast whirling spiral and hit the ground feet first at an estimated speed of from 50 to 75 feet per second—roughly 34 to 52 miles an hour.

By some miracle, Lujano was still alive, conscious and coherent when rescuers reached his side. Rushed to a hospital, he died within two hours from multiple frac-tures and internal injuries. Investigators deduced that the malfunction was "caused by bad body position during ripcord pull and further complicated by improper de-ployment of the reserve."

Blown-out panels or tears in the canopy are not neces-sarily unsafe. Large holes or too many of them will in-crease a jumper's rate of descent, however. Most para-chutists will release their reserve chutes if the main canopy appears damaged or tangled at all, regardless of the extent.

Generally the emergency or reserve pack is carried without a pilot chute, thus enabling the jumper to control deployment and avoid having it engage with the main canopy, as in the case of Louie Lujano. To open the auxiliary, the jumper holds the pack closed with his left arm, pulls the ripcord with his right hand, then grabs the folded canopy and throws it away from his body. As it inflates, he feeds out the stowed lines.

The majority of all parachuting mishaps are attribu-table to one of several probable causes—complete failure to pull the ripcord on either the main chute or the re-serve, improper opening position resulting in malfunc-tions, uncontrolled free fall and, oddly enough, drowning.

An analysis of some 65 sport-parachuting fatalities tabulated from 1958 through 1963 shows that failure to pull or pulling the ripcord too late accounted for the greatest percentage. Next were malfunctions coupled

Two sky sailors of the Navy parachute team are seconds from completing a baton pass as they drop through space at breath-taking speeds. They began to fall at 12,500 feet. (*U.S. Navy*)

with failure to activate the reserve or with improper deployment of the reserve.

Other causes include midair collisions, faulty equipment, accidental reserve chute opening inside the aircraft, improper canopy manipulation, and inadvertent release of both "Capewells" in the air—the quick disconnect devices which attach the main parachute lift webs to the harness.

PCA safety specialists are unable to pin down the specific mental, physical, or mechanical problem in every fatal accident, especially when experienced jumpers are involved. However, students account for about 85 per cent of all skydiving fatalities. PCA states that "in almost every fatality there was an element or moment of carelessness, an oversight or an indifference on the part of either the jumper or the supervisor."

Why some jumpers fail to pull either ripcord is often impossible to explain. A jumper can become disoriented if he remains out of control too long in free fall. Or he might suffer redout as a result of rapid body rotation or spinning. Other factors known to affect the parachutist's ability to function properly are two potential killers—hypoxia and hyperventilation.

Either condition might have been a contributing cause in Robert J. Gardner's death at the Santa Ynez, California, Jumpers Jamboree over the 1963 Labor Day weekend. Gardner and 28 other skydivers had gone up in two airplanes for a mass nighttime leap from 15,000 feet. Each jumper carried red flares to trace his descent in a spectacular fire-fall trail. All landed safely but Gardner, whose parachute had just started to open when he hit the ground.

Hypoxia is an oxygen deficiency in the blood, cells, and body tissues; hyperventilation is an excessive loss of carbon dioxide, a waste product needed in the human system to maintain the proper physiological balance. The effect of hypoxia begins to develop around 10,000 feet and increases with altitude, ultimately leading to unconsciousness and death.

Hyperventilation, on the other hand, is brought on by breathing hard and fast to offset oxygen starvation. But one cannot be traded for the other. If the jumper breathes rapidly in an effort to "store up" extra oxygen, the carbon dioxide level in the lungs will go below normal. Should the jumper continue to hyperventilate for any length of time, he will experience numbness, dizziness, even brief loss of consciousness.

All drownings reported to PCA during the past five years could have been avoided by better preparation. One man who jumped into the water intentionally wore a life vest but failed to inflate it. In the other cases adequate lifesaving gear and boats at landing sites would have saved jumpers. High-tension lines have also claimed a few lives.

A freak Memorial Day accident in 1963 near Liberty, Missouri, killed Karl Dean Frandsen when he hit a moving freight train at the edge of Moseby Airport.

Frandsen, a member of the Mid America Skydivers with many successful leaps, jumped from 4,500 feet. As he neared the surface, a sudden gust of wind caught his chute and carried him toward the railroad tracks. He landed hard on top of a boxcar, bounced about 15 feet into the air over it, and came to rest in a crumpled heap on an adjacent embankment. He died later.

All this attention to accidents has but one purpose: to stress the vital importance of proper training, equipment, and procedures in all sport-parachuting operations. To say that parachuting can be just as safe as the participant cares to make it isn't quite true, either. When man flies or dives through the sky, he is invading an unnatural element. As a result, there are certain very formidable physical forces that attack him.

Yet, by many standards, parachuting today is one of the safest contact sports in the world. FAA's chief concern, of course, is its fantastic rate of growth and its relation to safety now and in the future.

PCA membership alone has increased by leaps and bounds, and it comprises only half of all the nation's active sport jumpers. Assuming that each of the 7,500 PCA members made a conservative 10 jumps in 1963, this would total 75,000 leaps. Double that figure to allow for all the non-PCA members in the United States and you have 150,000 sport leaps over a single 12-month period.

Moreover, if Deke Sonnichsen's prediction of 35,000 PCA members by 1970 comes true, the total number of jumps in one year could easily approach three-quarters of a million!

This is why PCA is so insistent on the physical, repetitive drilling of student jumpers by highly qualified instructors. PCA also issues various classes of licenses denoting different levels of parachuting experience and skills, but only after methodical review and verification of the applicant's jumping record. The licenses are actually conferred by the Fédération Aéronautique Internationale, following PCA's approval and endorsement.

FAI, founded in 1905 and now an organization of more than 50 member nations, governs all world aeronautical sport, including parachuting. Its United States representative, the National Aeronautic Association (NAA), sanctions and controls all official aviation sporting contests and record trials in America. As a nonprofit division of NAA, the Parachute Club of America manages all sanctioned parachuting activities and licensing in the United States.

The FAI-NAA-PCA rating system for certification of parachute jumpers begins with "student parachutist." As defined by PCA, a student parachutist is any person with less than 25 free, delayed falls. He may qualify for a United States FAI Class A license.

After the student logs 25 or more free falls, including delays of up to at least 30 seconds, he can qualify for Class B and the loftier designation of parachutist. The United States FAI Class B license holder is capable of briefing the pilot, selecting his exit point, and jumping without supervision in accordance with PCA safety rules. He may also make demonstration and relative-work jumps and serve as a local parachute club safety officer.

United States FAI Class C parachutists must have completed a minimum of 75 delayed jumps, including free falls of 60 seconds or more. They are qualified to supervise training and jumping operations as jump-masters and to make demonstration, night, water, and relative leaps. They may also try for official records.

Jumpers holding Class C licenses are deemed competent parachutists. They are eligible for PCA's instructor rating and for appointment as an area safety officer.

The highest international grade is the United States FAI Class D license which requires at least 200 free falls, including delays of a minute or more. PCA designates the Class D jumper as an expert parachutist who may do all the things authorized in the lower grades, as well as to instruct in parachuting, provided he adheres to all club doctrines and precepts.

PCA also issues a parachute-instructor rating to jumpers who complete requirements in excess of Class C minimums and pass a comprehensive written, oral, and practical test. Although the PCA instructor rating is not an FAI license, applicants must have at least a valid Class C or D ticket.

One of the rated PCA parachute instructor's primary duties is to certify the qualifications of applicants for United States FAI Class A, B, C, and D licenses. His instructor rating is good until revoked, unlike the FAI licenses, which have annual minimum-experience requirements. However, the instructor is expected to keep his own United States FAI license valid. Like all other license holders, he does this by registering the required jumps each year.

As in most rigidly controlled fields of endeavor, there are inspectors checking the inspectors. In skydiving, they are called examiners, and are officials named by PCA to administer the parachute-instructor examination. The designation is relatively new, not having been created until February, 1962.

On the regional level, the PCA area safety officer is the primary judicial authority. Appointed on the basis of personal integrity, judgment, and knowledge of the sport, the ASO is entrusted with the direct supervision and surveillance of parachuting activities within an assigned geographic territory. He also verifies license applications, corrects and reports safety violations, investigates accidents, and works closely with local clubs. He must also hold at least a United States FAI Class C license.

The number of certified leaps in a jumper's logbook is only one criterion for licensing. The higher the rating, the tougher the requirements.

Depending on the class license, applicants must demonstrate a variety of skydiving skills, such as long stable falls, tracking, night and water jumps, precision turns, landing accuracy, and other maneuvers that come only with practical experience. In addition, all persons engaged in parachuting under the aegis of PCA must meet certain qualifications for physical fitness.

As this is written, the only Federal Aviation Agency license required in parachuting is that of parachute rigger. Anyone who packs a reserve chute for premeditated jumping or personnel (air crew) equipment for emergency use in civil aircraft must hold an appropriate current parachute rigger certificate as prescribed in Federal Air Regulation Part 65.

These FAA certificates are issued with ratings covering specific types of parachutes that the licensee may pack, such as seat, back, chest, or special-purpose parachute. Requirements include passing a written examination and a practical demonstration of packing competence for each rating. Oddly, there are fewer than 3,500 certificated riggers in the country despite the rapidly increasing numbers of active jumpers.

Sport parachutists may pack their own main chutes, whether they are FAA-licensed or not. Generally most of them pack their own, but only after learning how from a qualified rigger.

Parachute packing is an art. However, the notion that it demands the skilled hands of a surgeon and facilities as immaculately clean as an operating room is a little far-fetched. If a conventional packing table is not available, the chute can easily be packed on any flat surface, such as a hangar floor, airport ramp, lawn, or hotel corridor.

All parachutes are packed essentially the same way, varying only slightly in the external rigging and the in-ternal placement of risers, lines, canopy, and pilot chute. Standard packing tables are about 40 feet long and at least 30 inches wide. If the work is to be done on the floor or ground, it's best first to lay out a packing mat of roughly the same dimensions.

Preparing a parachute for use is actually a combination of inspecting, rigging, and packing. It requires special tools, and can be done best by two or three people work-ing as a team.

First, the parachute is stretched to its full length on the packing surface as if the wearer were on his back, head toward the canopy. Then the entire assembly is thoroughly inspected for any rips, tears, holes, stains, or other possible defects. Next, tension must be applied by drawing the parachute taut. If a regular table equipped with spreader bar and hook is not used, the desired tension can be obtained by having one person hold the canopy apex, and another the lift webs at the harness end.

Once taut, the parachute is straightened, lines checked, any tangles cleared, and the canopy whipped and folded to reduce its area by a series of neat, consecutive pleats. This step in the packing sequence is also known as flaking the canopy. The pleated canopy is then folded into thirds, lengthwise.

Next, tension is released, and the shroud, or suspension, lines are stowed by inserting them in rubber bands or nylon hesitator loops in the bottom of the pack tray. The folded canopy is placed on top of the stowed lines, accordion fashion, followed by the pilot chute. Container flaps are then pulled over the entire assembly to compress and close the pack. Finally, ripcord locking pins are inserted in their cones, elastic opening bands hooked up, and a protector flap fastened.

Parachutes using special deployment sleeves are packed in a little different manner. The sleeve slides over the folded canopy, from peak to skirt, completely encasing it. Next, suspension lines are stowed in place on the lower portion of the sleeve rather than in the container tray. And the pilot chute attaches to the sleeve bridle, instead of to the canopy apex.

The sleeve's function is to preload the entire deployment system—the orderly sequence of parachute activation—before the canopy inflates, thus reducing opening

Twin pilot chutes, acting as an air anchor, pull the main canopy from the pack of one United States Army Golden Knight as his teammate's parachute begins to inflate. (*Joe M. Gonzales*)

shock. Another deployment device is the full or partial bag. It is similar to the sleeve, except that the canopy accordion-folds within the bag.

Many veteran parachutists, while conceding certain obvious advantages, warn that using sleeves or bags increases the possibility of malfunctions. That their good features outweigh the bad is apparent by the wide popularity of such systems.

Parachute Club of America directors constantly review jumping practices and membership behavior. Periodically they find it necessary to make sweeping changes in policies and procedures for a more equitable and workable management of the sport, all in the public interest as well as PCA's.

In line with efforts aimed at upgrading sport parachuting by developing better guidance for members, PCA recently overhauled all operating parameters. As a result, the club adopted a whole new set of completely revised safety regulations and a new training doctrine, both effective November 1, 1963.

For organizational purposes, PCA has divided the United States into a dozen geographic "conference areas" or zones. Each area selects its own conference director who also complements the nationally elected members on PCA's governing board. This grass-roots representation assures the membership of an effective voice in national club affairs. PCA founder Joe Crane became the club's first board chairman.

Implemented for the first time in June, 1963, the new conference-director concept, plus expanded local, regional, and national competitions, should build a solid foundation for the sport's continued growth. And it will, if jumpers now and in the future maintain acceptable accident levels.

CHAMPIONS AND SHOWMEN 7

THERE ARE A NUMBER OF REASONS WHY THE BIG SIXTH
World Sport Parachuting Championships held in the
summer of 1962 at Orange, Massachusetts, are destined
to become a part of aviation history.

To begin with, the competition was the largest international aeronautical contest ever staged in the Western
Hemisphere. And this includes the colorful old air meets
that brought many countries together in a bygone era,
such as the vintage James Gordon Bennett, the Schneider,
and the Pulitzer trophy races.

When the dust settled at Orange, the United States
had emerged as an indisputable world power in sport
parachuting. It captured three first-place victories out of
four events and finished a close second in the fourth and
final test.

All told, 25 nations represented by more than 300
jumpers vied in the competitions which ran from August
11 to September 3, 1962. For over three weeks Orange,
a pleasant, tranquil little town rich in quaint New England tradition, resembled some sort of United Nations

Bull's-eye landings were once a rarity in parachuting, but in competition today at least one dead-center impact is the rule, rather than the exception. Often, several are made. (*Joe M. Gonzales*)

experiment in coexistence. The Ralph C. Mahar Regional High School became "Friendship Lodge"—home of participating teams where the sounds of many languages echoed through crowded halls and rooms.

Orange transformed amateur precision jumpers into

professional showmen. Competitive parachuting today is one of the most important organized activities of every local club. Each stages its own periodic competitions for members of all levels of experience. The club's best jumpers also compete in regional and conference-area contests. Just about every skydiver who can qualify has his or her sights set on the annual national championships and a place on the official United States parachute team.

First formal international parachuting competitions were held right after World War I, primarily as a method of proving the best parachute design from several different types entered.

France was the scene of several early evaluation trials. In the Nieuport-Astra contest in 1919, a pretty woman jumper named Marian Collins wearing a Jean Ors parachute competed against men using a new Froidure pack, one of the very earliest models to incorporate a pilot chute.

Even in those days motion pictures recorded parachute deployment sequences and opening times. As most competition jumps of the period were made from balloons, the cameraman would go aloft either with the parachutist or in another balloon in close proximity to accomplish his air-to-air photography.

In the United States, Lieutenant A. G. Hamilton claimed the world's first *official* altitude record for a parachute drop in 1920, although a year later Sergeant Ralph Bottriel's leap from 20,500 feet in a test project proved to be about 500 feet higher.

Until Joe Crane created formal contests for landing accuracy in the 1926 National Air Races, most public parachuting displays in the United States were billed as "death-defying" exhibitions. Occasionally in the early twenties a major air meet would feature some form of jumping competitions, but wild aerobatic flying and plane racing always monopolized every scheduled program.

We have seen that world parachuting championship competitions under Fédération Aéronautique Internationale auspices began in 1951 when five countries jumped against each other in Yugoslavia. France, where jumping had already become a national sport, walked off with top honors, Pierre Lard winning the men's crown and Monique La Roche the women's title.

The second world championships in 1954, at Saint Yans, France, signaled a turning point in international competitions. Won by Ivan Fetchichin, a talented Soviet parachutist who averaged about five yards from target in the landing accuracy contest, this meet introduced free-fall events as a regular program feature. Style consisted chiefly of body control and ability to open within a tenth of a second of a specified time.

International parachuting championships were now established as a biennial event sanctioned every even year by FAI.

Perhaps the third world meet in 1956 produced the greatest change in the complexion of sport parachuting.

The 1956 biennial meet was held in Moscow, and

Russia demonstrated a new parachute. It was actually a refinement of an earlier model and had blank (open) gores and steering toggles. The new canopy proved more stable and controllable than any other equipment then in production.

This unique parachute led United States designers to develop the concept of lift effect in competition canopies. Slots in the canopy are cut out and positioned in a way that reduces horizontal speed caused by wind drift, and at the same time reduce the rate of descent. Moreover, the oscillation factor is virtually eliminated as a real hazard. It all adds up to less landing shock. This same principle is applied to certain types of emergency parachutes and space-vehicle recovery systems.

Another innovation seen in Moscow was a Soviet modification of a German-designed deployment system —the sleeve, a pillowcase-like affair for retarding the parachute opening.

In the early forties several Navy parachute riggers at Lambert Field in St. Louis constructed sleeves for use in a series of free-fall demonstrations. Theirs differed from modern designs in that the suspension lines were stowed directly on the pack tray, as in a standard container. Still, the old sleeves completely enclosed the entire parachute canopy just like the ones in use today.

Oddly enough, until recently the free-fall French jumpers were prohibited from using sleeves by some arbitrary regulation, even though France has always been one of the most progressive nations in parachuting. (In the 1930's France trained volunteer nurses in the techniques of parachuting to wounded, while encouraging civil jumping as a popular pastime.)

Fourteen nations sent parachutists to the Fourth World Sport Parachuting Championships in 1958 at Bratislavia, Czechoslovakia, where Russia regained the world title she had lost in 1956. And repeating its performance of two years before, the United States again came in sixth.

By now parachute design had undergone substantial changes; and the standards for landing accuracy were within two yards of the target center. At the 1958 meet, for the first time, the parachutist had to make a split decision in free fall. After five seconds of delay, a ground signal gave the contestant an option of three series of maneuvers.

The jumper competing in the style event faces a test much like that of the skier in a slalom race. He must perform certain maneuvers swiftly and accurately, yet if he goes too fast he may lose control and irretrievable points.

United States Army parachutists made up the 1960 American team which traveled to the fifth international championships at Sofiya, Bulgaria, where it placed fourth. Russia successfully defended its world title in the 12-nation field, but James L. Arender brought home America's first gold medal—first place in the style event.

In overall point standings, Dick Fortenberry of the United States team finished second to the new world champion, Czechoslovakia's Zdenek Kaplan.

Born in 1939 in Shawnee, Oklahoma, also the birthplace of Astronaut Leroy Gordon Cooper, Jim Arender typifies the all-American-boy image. He entered the Army after a year of college as a premed student, and by choice wound up in the 82nd Airborne Division.

In 1958 he became a member of the original Strategic Army Corps (STRAC) parachute team formed at Fort Bragg. And two years later he participated in America's first successful six-man baton pass from 30,000 feet. By the time he had fulfilled his military obligation, Jim Arender had won a host of parachuting awards and honors.

As a civilian, Arender competed as a member of the United States team in the 1961 international invitational meet at La Ferté-Gaucher, France. The team swept all five first-place trophies, the best showing ever made by an American team in world parachuting up to that time.

Probably Jim Arender's most significant triumph so far in competition was winning the world overall parachuting championship in the men's division at the 1962 international event in Orange, Massachusetts.

There were five major titles to be competed for in the Sixth World Sport Parachuting Championships, plus individual and team winners of the five events. Because of bad weather, only four of the five scheduled contests were completed for women and three of the five for men. Czechoslovakia, achieving the highest point total score for both men and women in the competition, emerged as overall world champion for 1962.

United States jumpers finished second to Czechoslo-

vakia in overall point standings. Russia, defending world
champion, was third. It was a milestone in our parachuting history as the United States returned to a position of
leadership in world aeronautical competitions.

Other participating nations included France, Canada,
Bulgaria, Yugoslavia, Poland, Romania, Spain, Great
Britain, Austria, Israel, Belgium, New Zealand, Ireland,
Switzerland, West Germany, Australia, Netherlands,
India, Saudi Arabia, South Korea, South Africa, and
Japan.

Not all were able to field complete men's and women's
teams; four countries—South Africa, South Korea, Japan,
and India—had only one representative. Saudi Arabia, not
an FAI member, was allowed to enter as a "competing
observer."

Around a huge earthen arena, especially constructed
at Orange for this remarkable tourney, flew the multi-
hued flags of the 25 different countries. Every day of the
meet this tremendous drop zone, 220 yards in diameter,
and appropriately named the "Friendship Bowl," was
rimmed by thousands of admiring spectators.

From the beginning of the sixth world tournament at
Orange, two things were immediately apparent. The
caliber of international competitors has greatly improved, and the Western nations have become a real
match for Russian and satellite countries which had
paced sport parachuting for so many years.

Generally, international meets are based on three individual events and an individual overall score, plus one

Jumpers must move from the target quickly as others approach during team landing contests. Here the *fichet*, a French word for the man who marks the contact points, scores a jump. (*Joe M. Gonzales*)

or two team events. The individual events are further broken down into two landing-accuracy competitions and one style contest. The team events are scored on the team average for landing accuracy. In scoring individual accuracy and style events, the parachutist is credited with a number of points when he goes up to jump. He will then *lose* points for incorrect or inferior performance.

In the first accuracy event, the parachutist has 200 points when he enters the airplane. He is expected to jump a height of 1,000 meters or 3,300 feet with a free fall up to 10 seconds from time of exit until the parachute opens. He will lose 10 points for exceeding the 10 seconds of delay *and* about two points for each meter he lands away from the target center. Three of four jumps are scored in this event.

The second accuracy event is judged in much the same way, though now the jumping altitude is 1,500 meters (5,400 feet). The jumper delays up to 21 seconds. He loses 50 points for opening his parachute prior to the fifteenth or after the twenty-first second. His landing is also scored as in the first event.

Probably the most exciting and exacting competition, from the viewpoint of both contestant and spectator, is the style event. Here the parachutist also boards the plane with 200 points to his credit. He leaps from 2,000 meters (6,600 feet) and is graded on the proficiency and precision of his style and maneuvering ability during free fall. He loses nothing on landing, however, no matter what his distance from target.

The style contestant departs his aircraft on a fixed signal from the ground. After he leaves the plane, another visual ground signal—displayed for five seconds—indicates one of three predetermined series of maneuvers or figures the jumper must perform. He must then execute in proper sequence 360-degree turns and back loops as fast and as smoothly as possible—within 20 seconds.

A bonus of five points goes to the jumper for every second he shaves from the prescribed time limit. In other words, if he completes the maneuver series in 17 seconds he gets 15 extra points. But he will *lose* 10 points for each second after the 20th second.

In the style event, points are also deducted during the maneuvers for failing to complete turns or loops, overshooting the figures, exceeding 30 seconds of delay, and so forth.

Team contests are judged on landing accuracy only. All jump distances from target center are averaged to compute the team's total score, based on the best two out of three group leaps. There are two team events in both men's and women's divisions—one from 1,000 meters (3,300 feet), the other from 1,500 meters (5,400 feet).

Individual winners are determined by the highest number of points scored in each event. Next, the individual scores in the accuracy and style events are added together; the jumper having the highest grand total then becomes the world's *overall* sport-parachuting champion for that year.

To determine the international team standings, team points are combined with the total scores of the four best men and three best women in the individual events. Czechoslovakia, for example, accumulated 11,039.426 points to edge out the United States by less than 32 points for the 1962 world title. And third-place Russia finished 137 points behind the United States team.

Gérard Trèves of France won the 1962 men's accuracy event from 1,000 meters by scoring an almost impossible 592 out of 600 points and by averaging less than a meter (about 39 inches) from dead center in three landings.

While Evenij Tkachenko of Russia dethroned Jim Arender as style champion, the skilled American captured second place just a half-point in front of another Soviet jumper, Oleg Kazakov. That Arender scored high enough in every event he entered to win the coveted world's overall championship was more than ample consolation for him for losing his style title by only six points.

Seven dead-center landings were made at Orange against only two in five previous world championships. A splendid Canadian team led by architect Daryl Henry broke the world group-landing accuracy record for four men from 1,500 meters with an average distance of 1.76 meters off target center. The United States squad also bettered the existing mark, but not Canada's jump, as Loy Brydon and Gerald Bourquin scored the only two consecutive dead-center landings ever made in competition.

Daryl Henry, prolific exponent of parachuting, believes that for a man to meet the challenge of the sky in competition, he must first learn to master himself.

The goal of the competitive parachutist, in Henry's view, should be the full realization of personal potential —the best performance of the individual who, in an alien environment, competes against nature as well as his fellow man. This requires complete elimination of any emotional distractions, and intense concentration of all rational and physical energies.

A University of Toronto graduate and former con-

stable with the Royal Canadian Mounted Police, Daryl
Henry has been jumping since 1959. He held the title of
Canadian national sport-parachuting champion for three
years, and placed sixth in the overall point standings in
the 1962 world meet.

In winning the overall men's championship, Jim
Arender scored 1,060.551 points. Vaclav Klima of
Czechoslovakia placed second with 1,052.914 points, and
Richard Fortenberry, also of the United States, finished
third with 1,051.630.

The results of the women's competitions were equally
close, with an American mother of two daughters becoming 1962 overall women's champion of the world.
Mrs. Muriel Simbro, of Van Nuys, California, whose
husband Henry served as an alternate for the United
States men's team, piled up 1,206.968 points to win top
honors. Dagmar Kuldova, Czechoslovakia, came in second with 1,202.699 points, and Mrs. Nona Pond, United
States, wife of a prominent jumper, placed third with
1,181.042.

Until recent years men seldom discussed the role of
women in parachuting, except perhaps in a critical way,
similar to their comments about female drivers. Most
male jumpers had a mistrust of the intrusion of women in
what they considered man's domain.

But women have been parachuting almost as long as
men. André Garnerin's pretty niece Eliza became the
world's first woman jumper when she leaped out of a

balloon basket with one of her uncle's contraptions near Paris in 1815.

Women swinging under a parachute were a familiar sight at county fairs and carnivals long before many people saw their first flying machine. Tiny Broadwick barnstormed all over the United States and Canada, jumping from both balloons and airplanes, between the years 1908 and 1922.

Ruth Garver might have succeeded Miss Broadwick as America's sky queen, but her exhibition career was ended when a parachute failed her at Wichita, Kansas, in 1924. She had made many jumps as a performer in her husband's flying circus which gained national fame in the early twenties.

Other women prominent in parachuting during the twenties included Billie Brown and Gene Du Rand, attractive girls who specialized in high- and low-altitude pulls. Another was Pearl White, who jumped first at Alexandria, Virginia, in 1928 and continued to perform exhibitions until she married in 1935. Today Pearl White Ward is active in the Civil Air Patrol.

Wanda Stralarski, Gretchen Reighard, Adeline Gray, and Ruth Allen were other well-known jumpers in the days leading up to World War II. A top precision free-fall artist of that era was Faye Lucille Cox, whose long-delayed jumps always wowed the crowds at the old National Air Races.

But as a group, women parachutists have come into

Portrait of the 1962 women's parachuting champion of the world, Muriel Simbro, a housewife and mother of two girls. Her husband, Henry Simbro, is also an outstanding jumper. (*Robert H. Buquor*)

their own only in recent years. Muriel Simbro, the 1962 world skydiving queen, has earned the unqualified respect of her male contemporaries. She became the first woman to qualify for a United States FAI Class D parachuting license and one of the first to exchange a baton with another jumper in midair.

"My personal reasons for learning to jump and for

continuing to learn changed as I progressed from the basic fundamentals to the intricacies of style, accuracy jumping, and relative work," Mrs. Simbro says. "I admit that most of my jumps are made with an eye toward international competition, for this is my final goal and my lasting reward."

Speaking to other women about the rewards of parachuting, however, Mrs. Simbro emphasizes the fun and enjoyment her whole family derives from the sport. She has found that for some, the pleasures are in carefree weekend fun jumping; for others, in the pursuit of skydiving excellence.

"Whatever your aim, wholehearted dedication will be the only way to find your goal," she adds.

Other women who are widely recognized for their skill in sport parachuting include Monique Gallimard of France, 1960 international champion; Vera Zouvoba, a leading Soviet jumper; and Czechoslovakia's Maria Stancikova, Dagmar Kuldova, Zdena Zarybnicka, and Eva Hribalova—winners of the 1962 style and individual accuracy events from 1,000 meters.

In one of the most stunning performances ever seen in world competition, United States women won the 1962 overall team championship of their division. Members of the squad were Muriel Simbro, Nona Pond, Carlyn Olson, and Kim Emmons.

Together they racked up 4,619.006 points to clinch the championship. Czechoslovakia's team finished second and Poland's third in women's overall standings.

Although the official world championships are held only on even-numbered years, there is at least one major international competition conducted annually. In 1963 there were two—the European Cup Meet at Leutkirch, Germany, and the now regularly scheduled Adriatic Cup Meet at Portorož, Yugoslavia. Tragically, Marica Baric, the attractive young women's parachuting champion of Yugoslavia, was killed practicing for the 1963 Adriatic meet. Miss Baric had competed at Orange in 1962.

At Leutkirch, a small farming village near the Bavarian Alps, the United States, represented by an all-Army team, triumphed over Spain, Austria, Germany, England, Switzerland, Ireland, and Belgium.

National competitions are staged yearly to crown the United States parachuting champions and select the top candidates for a new United States team. Based on results of the 1963 National Parachute Championships held in September at Seattle, the outstanding male and female competitors formed the nucleus of the official 1964 United States Parachute Team.

The 1963 national champions were Dick Fortenberry of the United States Army, who won the men's title for the third straight year, and Anne Batterson of Bloomfield, Connecticut, who scored the first dead-center landing ever recorded by a woman in the annual national competitions.

When the new United States team was finally chosen, it immediately began weeks of rugged drilling for the

Seventh World Sport Parachuting Championships set for August, 1964, in West Germany.

The Parachute Club of America conducts national team tryouts each year so that the United States will always field its best talent in any international competition. To compete in national championships, the men must hold a valid FAI Class D license and the women a Class C or higher ticket. Eligible contestants must also belong to PCA.

There are five major objectives of world championship competitions: the award of individual and team titles, establishment of new international records, popularization of parachuting, the exchange of experience and knowledge acquired in this growing sport, and the strengthening of friendships between participating countries of both hemispheres.

> "For I dipt into the future,
>   far as human eye could see,
> Saw the Vision of the world,
>   and all the wonders that would be;
> Saw the heavens fill with commerce,
>   argosies of magic sails,
> Pilots of the purple twilight,
>   dropping down with costly bales . . ."

THESE PROPHETIC LINES FROM TENNYSON'S IMMORTAL "Locksley Hall," written in 1842 (exactly 120 years before the world parachuting championships at Orange), correctly anticipated the scientific marvels that were to come decades later.

By the year 1970 a cluster of three enormous ringsail parachutes, each 88 feet in diameter, will gently lower to earth the NASA three-man Apollo spacecraft returning from a two-week voyage to the moon, some 240,000 miles distant. Yet to get this remarkable vehicle down safely with its precious human cargo, modern science

will depend upon an umbrella-like device first sketched
by a gifted Italian painter nearly five hundred years ago.

The parachute forms the heart of current space-
vehicle recovery systems. It is one of the most vital of
many interdependent elements whose perfect functioning is necessary for successful completion of a space
mission.

To single out any system as the one most responsible
for bringing man back safely from space is like saying
which tooth in a saw cut the log. The importance of the

Three American astronauts returning from
moon flight in a NASA Apollo spacecraft
will be landed by Northrop Ventura's system of three 88-foot ringsail parachutes, as
shown in this test.

parachute to reliable recovery is evident from the fact it has held major system status in spacecraft design from the very beginning.

In the Apollo mission, recovery will start after the lunar flight as the spacecraft's command module reenters the earth's atmosphere at a searing 25,000 miles per hour. The cone-shaped vehicle containing the three astronauts will decelerate as the forces of friction build up in denser air. When it is 25,000 feet above earth a conical ribbon drogue chute will be ejected automatically by a mortar blast.

The drogue chute stabilizes and slows the spacecraft to a terminal velocity satisfactory for deployment of the main parachute without danger of rupturing the material.

Each of the three main ringsail parachutes will be deployed by a pilot chute mortared out independently but simultaneously with the other two at 15,000 feet. The main chute canopies will then open fully between 14,000 and 13,500 feet from the ground.

Use of three parachutes provides a safety factor that makes the system its own backup unit. Two chutes will lower the Apollo command module at a rate of 33 feet per second, while the full cluster of three slow the descent to a pleasant 24 feet.

For the Mercury capsule, flown successfully by six American astronauts, a six-foot ribbon chute deployed at 21,000 feet to start the landing sequence. It stabilized the falling spacecraft, and acted as a pilot chute to extract the main 63-foot ringsail at about 10,000 feet.

Gemini, a two-man spacecraft, will require a single 84-foot main parachute. Its recovery system may also incorporate a novel inflatable flexwing—a kite-like apparatus similar in shape to the paper airplanes children fold—which would enable the astronauts to land Gemini on skids, as a glider. And instead of an escape tower for low-altitude aborts, Gemini has two ejection seats like those used in jets.

Although it was not generally publicized, each Mercury astronaut carried his own backup recovery system—a quickly attached chest parachute.

Unlike Soviet cosmonauts, the American astronauts did not land by individual parachute. But to prepare for the two-man Gemini space flights, astronauts were drilled in the techniques of parachute landings during a survival training course in the fall of 1963.

Interest in developing parachute equipment capable of lowering unusually heavy loads actually dates back to World War I. The first widely publicized test occurred in March, 1921, when the Italian Department of Aeronautical Construction dropped a touring car under a new Nobile parachute released from a balloon at 1,000 feet. The automobile landed without damage.

E. L. Hoffman, Jimmy Russell, and other designers experimented with large airplane parachutes in the late twenties and early thirties. Their tests proved that the idea would work, though it was never adopted.

More dramatic proof came as recently as the summer of 1963, when Walter Chionni, a French skydiver, leaped from a plane near Fréjorgue, France, in what he had planned as a routine sport jump. For some reason the chute burst open prematurely, and the shroud lines tangled in the airplane's tail. The snarl caused pilot Christian de la Beaume to lose control; the biplane fell off on a wing and started spinning.

Chionni instinctively pulled his reserve chute, which billowed open alongside his main canopy. All three—pilot, parachutist, and plane—floated 2,500 feet to earth, suffering only one broken leg and a slightly banged-up airplane.

Italy is still pioneering in king-size parachutes. A plant in Perugia manufactures a mammoth canopy measuring 100 yards across—the length of a football field—and 50 yards high. Perhaps the world's largest, the canopy and lines alone weigh 200 pounds. It will lower armored trucks, a complete field hospital unit, or emergency supplies for 2,000 persons in a single drop. It can be called an extension of Italy's tests with the Nobile parachute of 1921.

The use of such an old aviation tool as the parachute does not mean that space-recovery technology is lagging, however. It is simply that parachutes are still the best recovery devices available because they provide the greatest amount of drag for their weight and are the most reliable, and the most versatile.

Aerospaceplanes, when operational, will not mark the end of parachute descents from space, say recovery experts. They point to the aerospaceplane's 35 per cent weight penalty, because of the aerodynamic surfaces and power needed to make the craft fly, compared to less than 15 per cent for the parachute retrieval system.

Most authorities agree that there will always be a need for vertical or gliding parachute-type landing systems; there will always be unmanned as well as manned vehicles to be recovered, such as cargo carriers, rocket boosters, instrument packages, and so forth.

The inflatable, flexible wing or paraglider concept pioneered by F. M. Rogallo for manned spacecraft might even be adapted in the future to Army airborne troops. Experimental models of the individual drop glider (IDG) system have already undergone extensive testing.

The IDG wing has 300 square feet of surface area and a keel 22 feet long. Also shaped like a paper airplane, it suspends the wearer in a manner similar to that of conventional parachutes. When the jumper leaps, a static line initiates wing deployment. After a preset time period, a compressed-air bottle triggers to inflate the keel and wing leading edges. During the rest of the descent, the jumper controls direction of the IDG by pulling on risers.

Ryan Aeronautical Company, builder of the test wings for the Army, believes the new IDG wing will provide an "off-set delivery capability and accuracy not obtainable with parachutes." Ryan further states that a man jumping at 10,000 feet will be able to guide himself to a target seven horizontal miles away.

Although the parachute has been around for centuries,

few people—including many skydivers—are fully aware of the amazing transformation it has undergone in recent years. Parachute technology, spurred by supersonic jets and the space age, now has a solid position in aeronautical engineering and science. As one expert puts it, "The time when parachutes were part of the garment industry is gone."

Great strides in the development of high-performance military aircraft since World War II have brought new problems in escape-system design.

According to Colonel John P. Stapp of the United States Air Force Aeromedical Laboratory, the ram effect of air at low altitude produces high resistance to ejection at high speeds. Resistance near sea level in ejection at Mach 1.4 would be the same as that of ejection at 100,000 feet and at Mach 14. (Mach numbers measure velocity

Early ejection-seat tests like this one from a Lockheed TV-2 in 1954 challenged the boldest parachutists. Later experiments led to more sophisticated systems for supersonic escape. (*U.S. Navy*)

in multiples or fractions of the speed of sound. Mach 14 equals 14 times the speed of sound.)

So the survival experts must develop ejection devices that will protect aircrews from the crushing forces of high-speed bailouts at all operational altitudes.

Before World War II most emergencies in flight would occur at speeds and altitudes that presented no real obstacle in jumping from disabled aircraft. But midway through the war a survey revealed that 12.5 per cent of emergency parachute jumps from new types of military planes were fatal—and more than 45 per cent involved serious injuries.

Probing further, the fact finders learned that most bailout casualties resulted from collision with the aircraft structure. Thus it was obvious that to avoid striking part of his own plane, the flyer would have to be catapulted out of the cockpit.

German engineers had been working on the ejection-seat principle since 1939. By the end of 1944 two revolutionary German aircraft were in service the Messerschmitt Me163 rocket-powered interceptor and twin-engine Me262, the world's first operational jet fighter. Both featured ejection seats. In less than a year Germany recorded 60 seat ejections.

In 1945 Sweden installed ejection seats in its J-21 fighter, and England tested the new Martin-Baker model with great success. Soon the United States Navy tried the British design, Lieutenant (jg) A. J. Furtek becoming the first American to eject in a Martin-Baker seat on October 30, 1949, at Lakehurst, New Jersey.

Research in the field of high-speed escape is never static. As solutions are found, along come new aircraft capable of flying higher and faster, and with them come new problems.

Almost daily at the risk of their own lives, heroic men of the Department of Defense Joint Parachute Test Facility at El Centro, California, evaluate new designs, techniques, and materials in aircrew escape systems. Much of the Mercury, Gemini, and Apollo recovery systems was developed and tested by these dedicated Air Force and Navy servicemen.

To review all the important firsts in parachute evolution would require another book, but several do merit mention here.

Sydney Hughes of the Royal Air Force, on August 28, 1957, made the first live, ground-level escape demonstration in the United States. This courageous airman ejected in a Martin-Baker seat from a Navy F9F-8T which never left the runway until Hughes shot out of the rear cockpit like the circus daredevil from a cannon. He was still hurtling through the air almost horizontally when his chute popped open. He swung down and landed unhurt.

On February 28, 1962, USAF Chief Warrant Officer Edward J. Murray became the first man to test a new rocket-powered escape capsule for the supersonic B-58 Hustler jet bomber.

Resembling an aluminum cocoon five feet high, two feet wide, and weighing about 700 pounds, its design marked a giant step forward in escape-system sophistication. Strapped inside it, Murray ejected from a B-58 flying 565 miles per hour at 20,000 feet. He accelerated vertically to 15 times the force of gravity and attained a top speed of 250 feet per second during a free fall of approximately 5,000 feet.

George F. Smith, a North American Aviation test pilot, is the first man known to survive a supersonic emergency bailout. It happened February 26, 1955, off Palos Verdes, California.

Flying a new F-100A, Smith suddenly felt the controls lock. The heavy fighter nosed over and plunged toward the sea. Triggering the ejection seat, Smith blew out at 6,500 feet and at a speed of 777 miles per hour.

Instantly, a supersonic brick wall slammed Smith unconscious. Luckily, however, the wind blast separated the pilot from his seat, and an aneroid device automatically released his parachute. Fishermen pulled the battered airman from the water more dead than alive. But he survived to fly again.

Doctors and engineers learned a lot from Smith's brush with death. Ejection seats were soon improved to provide greater protection for jet pilots.

Colonel William H. Rankin of the Marine Corps made one of the most astounding parachute jumps on record. One turbulent night in July, 1959, Rankin was forced to abandon his F8U Crusader at 47,000 feet. He was not wearing a pressure suit. He tumbled to 10,000 feet, and there a barometric sensor opened his parachute.

The colonel's feeling of relief lasted about a second. Almost immediately after the canopy inflated, he was sucked up into a raging thunderstorm. Tornadic winds ripped at his clothing and slapped his parachute closed, then blew it open again. Hailstones the size of golf balls pounded his body.

Rankin's descent should have taken less than 10 minutes—but it took more than 40.

Just as pioneer airmen rejected the first parachutes, their modern counterparts voiced strong opposition to the early ejection seats. Jet pilots realized that the catapulting action required a cartridge comparable in force to a 20-millimeter shell. And like any loaded gun, under certain conditions an accidental firing could kill or cripple.

There have been cases of explosive charges going off because of a malfunction of the actuating mechanism, some with tragic consequences. But progressive refinements have made the modern seat virtually foolproof, if properly installed and operated.

Research continues. The ejection seat is not the last word, nor is the encapsulated escape system which, as designed for the new biservice F-111 (TFX) fighter, already eclipses the B-58's in sophistication. For the F-111, a 50,000-pound thrust rocket motor propels the entire two-man crew compartment from the plane. At the proper time a main parachute opens automatically to lower the complete pod and its crew safely down.

New performance and environment parameters, complicated by even greater requirements for reliability, will combine to challenge the engineers of tomorrow.

Perhaps the new generation of pioneers will find inspiration in their legacy—a legacy of unrelenting human endeavor. Many brave men and women have shared in the achievements that continue to win for parachutes and parachuting greater acceptance in modern science, industry, and society.

It is an acceptance that was not easily won. It was a struggle against oft-seemingly insurmountable obstacles —the frail, unproved equipment of the early days, the natural hazards of unknown elements, and always the battle to overcome skepticism.

There was T. V. Pearson who pioneered a smoke-jumping program in 1933 because he thought it might help protect one of our nation's greatest natural resources. Finally, in 1940, parachuting fire fighters were formally organized as an arm of the Forest Service, with Rufus Robinson and Earl Cooley becoming the unit's first members. Today smoke jumpers are ready to leap anywhere that fire might threaten timberland.

With the elite paratroopers and paracommandos emerged the paramedics and the pararescue teams who jump under any condition to help save a life. The pararescue specialist is also trained to recover space capsules at sea or even in some remote, isolated area on land.

Certainly deserving of a large share of the credit for parachute development, application, and acceptance are the silk splitters—the professional exhibition jumpers of

Thrilling flag jumps, with plenty of smoke and noise from a circling stunt plane, still open many air-show programs. Here Jinx Gillespie descends under his Hoffman Triangle. (*James Yarnell*)

yesteryear. They were the forerunners of the modern skydiver, and a few of them form the hard core of sport parachuting today.

Joe Crane, father of parachute competitions, was perhaps the busiest of all the old pros who split silk any time a crowd of two or more people would gather to watch men defy gravity.

Crane and another jumper named Roger Don Rae,

who doubled as a racing pilot and who now flies jets for Trans World Airlines, waged a running battle for top money in parachute spot-landing contests at the old National Air Races. Another hot competitor of that era was Jerry Wessling, who died of a head injury after a hard landing on a concrete runway, and two others were the first real exponents of the controlled free fall—Steve Budreau and Spud Manning.

During the days of barnstorming, stunting, and record-making, the parachute jumper was usually billed as the star attraction. Every flying circus worth the price of an airplane ride featured wing walking, plane changing, and wild aerobatics at treetop altitude, but the delayed parachute jump as a grand finale always stole the show.

From cow pastures, fairgrounds and later from flying fields, the air show flourished far and wide in the "Golden Age of Aviation"—the period between two world wars. The original barnstormer was a product of World War I, yet he managed to endure through the lean depression years of the 1930's.

It is a good thing, too, for his exciting exploits helped create a public awareness of aviation as a way of life, as well as a powerful force. Modern air power as we know it today owes much to the pioneering barnstormer.

Recently there has been a resurgence of interest in the old-style air show. Antique airplanes, clown acts, wing riding, precision aerobatics, and plenty of smoke and noise—plus the parachute jump. These are the exciting acts being shown around the country by a few promoters bent on recapturing and perpetuating the color, romance, and adventure of America's proud heritage in the air.

Some of these air-show men like Bill Sweet, Duane Cole, and Bob McComb, have been in the business for years. Others are relatively newcomers. But all hope to keep the old flying circus alive in the best Ivan Gates-Clyde Pangborn tradition.

For some reason, many devotees of skydiving frown on professional exhibitions. Yet the only real distinction between exhibition jumping and "pure sport" parachuting is money.

Modern skydivers particularly object to the use of cloth extensions and other forms of simulated control surfaces that are designed to increase the parachutist's glide capability. Jumpers call these devices bat wings.

Clem Sohn is believed to have invented the idea of using canvas wing extensions to his coveralls. The innovation ultimately killed him. It also killed Leo Valentin, the much-vaunted "human bird" of France, who developed the idea further than any other jumper. Next to Sohn, a rugged professional named Tommy Boyd ranked at the top of the few American parachutists who used wing structures consistently.

Last of the American bat men was Roy "Red" Grant, who in 1962 climaxed 17 years of exhibition jumping by making two international "flights" on his canvas wings, from the United States to Canada and back over Niagara Falls.

But no parachute exhibition of the past or present, professional or amateur, can compare with the performances of two United States service teams—the Army's Golden Knights and the Navy's Chuting Stars.

These two official demonstration teams are making parachute history; their skill and showmanship rival anything ever put before a circus fan by Ringling Brothers, Barnum and Bailey.

In 1962 Roy "Red" Grant, noted "batman," celebrated seventeen years of exhibition jumping by making two flights on his canvas wings from the United States to Canada— over Niagara Falls.

Oldest in point of organization, the Army team was formed in 1958. In June, 1961, it received official status as a full-time parachute exhibition unit. Professionals in every sense of the word, the Golden Knights bear on their shields the proud motto *Altus et Validus*—"High and Mighty."

Based at Fort Bragg, the Army jumpers dive through the skies of nearly every state in the Union and over several foreign countries. No fewer than twenty million people witnessed their aerial gymnastics in a five-year period.

Team members have to their credit about 700 free-fall jumps each. Several have made over 1,200. They make most of their delays from 13,500 feet, their trails in space marked by brilliant plumes of colored smoke that flaunt from small grenades lashed to jump boots.

Keeping close check on their stop watches and altimeters, the Golden Knights open their parachutes around 1,500 feet up. Their black-and-gold canopies, the team trade-mark, are guided to pinpoint landings a few feet in front of the spectators. Then in the wink of an eye, the Knights shed harness, helmet, and a special drop-away suit to appear at parade rest in freshly pressed uniforms, as if ready for a general's inspection.

It's all part of the act, but this kind of precision performance is as stirring as that of the Air Force Thunderbirds and Navy Blue Angels flying teams.

One of the Army's most spectacular displays is the double cutaway patterned after an old flying-circus stunt of years ago. The parachutist leaps from 13,500 feet, falls in a stable-spread position for 11,000 feet, then deploys a 24-foot canopy. After a few seconds he collapses the chute, then cuts it away completely. At about 1,800 feet he opens a second parachute and repeats the procedure.

Finally, at about 1,300 feet the Golden Knight releases his regular black-and-gold main pack and drives toward his target.

The Army jumpers have a whole bag of heart-stopping tricks, including baton passes and incredible aerobatic maneuvers. They rank among the best free-fall experts in the world and have the records to prove it—no less than 48 international marks for landing accuracy.

Equally adept at spellbinding crowds, the Navy Chuting Stars were first organized in 1960, as a temporary unit to mark the Fiftieth Anniversary of Naval Aviation coming up the following year. Chief Warrant Officer Lewis

Sailing in on target, the parachutist strains to close his distance to dead center at lower right, where the scorer stands. *Fichets* rush to mark contact point. (*Joe M. Gonzales*)

Parachutists of the Navy Chuting Stars seem to be tumbling out of the jump plane, a Douglas R4D-8 (Super-DC-3), but they have already begun to assume stable-fall attitude. (*U.S. Navy*)

T. Vinson, one of the Navy's foremost test parachutists, and a recipient of the coveted Leo Stevens Award for his contributions to flying safety, was recalled from retirement to train the new team.

In its first season the Navy jumpers traveled over 52,000 miles to give 40 exhibitions before three million spectators. Then in July, 1961, the Chuting Stars were made a permanent unit assigned to the Home of Naval Aviation at Pensacola, Florida.

These skydiving sailors have four basic routines that begin when they leave their jump platform at 12,500 feet. They spend 60 seconds in free fall, swallowing over 10,000 feet of space before they pull their ripcords.

One routine sends two men arching gracefully past each other, then back again. Another includes four jumpers who leap in quick succession, swoop toward each other and then merge in a tight formation. After 40 seconds of delay they fire flare guns simultaneously as they separate, each taking up his own cardinal heading on the four compass points. Ten seconds later they double back, opening their chutes as they close in. They call this awesome maneuver the star burst.

In another maneuver, two Chuting Stars exchange a baton, not once but several times, as they glide toward earth. A final basic stunt, the double breakaway, involves two pairs of jumpers. Both pairs separate on the way down, reverse course and execute crossover figures in a diamond pattern.

There are alternate figures which the team members perform to demonstrate the high degree of control possible in a good skydive. One is designed to show the vast difference in the rates of free fall, while another proves that a jumper can travel almost one foot horizontally for every foot he drops vertically. It looks deceptively easy, but this kind of skydiving requires many weeks of training and practice.

Generally, members of Army and Navy teams have had previous experience as military or naval jumpers or as civilian parachutists. It is prestige duty; both teams have waiting lists that seldom fall below 25 men. There are only two or three vacancies a year to be filled on either team, however.

The development of dependable parachute devices for delivering men, materials, or machines safely from the skies represents a systematic progression that dates all the way back to Sebastian Lenormand's crude apparatus for escape from burning buildings.

Behind this remarkable growth are the many dedicated, determined, visionary people who shared an unshakable faith in the parachute as a useful, productive instrument for advancing man's knowledge and well-being . . . the Da Vincis, the Garnerins, the Cockings, the Broadwicks, the Hoffmans, the Smiths, the Cranes, the Vinsons, and the Kittingers—to name but a few. To them, the sky is every man's heritage.

In many quarters jumpers are still regarded as barnstorming stunt men. Yet in time the continued expansion of sport parachuting may dispel this impression. Skydiving is rapidly winning converts. No other form of outdoor recreational activity of recent years has grown quite so fast.

Parachuting is a kind of poetry in motion. To the practicing enthusiast, it transcends all other sporting experiences. There is beauty in free flight through space— a rhythmical exhilaration beyond all earthly rationalism. It stimulates man's inner thoughts, his keenly sensitive perception to the wonders, meaning, and depth of the universe around him.

Like intruders from outer space, three Navy Chuting Stars appear to soar over the misty mountains of southern California in a display symbolizing man's mastery of the skies. (*U.S Navy*)

In a way, the spirit of parachuting might best be summed up in the words of Edna St. Vincent Millay:

"The world stands out on either side,
no wider than the heart is wide;
Above the world is stretched the sky,
no higher than the soul is high."

About the Author

Jim Greenwood made his first airplane flight in 1936; two years later he was making parachute jumps. He logged 236 free-fall exhibition leaps before hanging up his harness for keeps in 1949.

The author has bailed out of everything from old biplanes to Navy transports. He performed air shows with some of the top names in the business, and admits to landing on or in places most parachutists avoid—trees, water, cattle, buildings, roads, power lines, brick piles, even an electric fence.

A licensed pilot, he once operated a commercial parachute service and taught jumping. He later directed publicity for the old Miami All American Air Maneuvers and became one of the National Aeronautic Association's first parachute contest stewards.

He has been a reporter, editor and feature writer. To obtain material for stories he flew through the eye of a hurricane, on a B-36 simulated bombing mission, and more recently in the slot position with the USAF *Thunderbirds* precision jet flying team. His first full-length book on jumping, *Parachuting for Sport*, was published in the summer of 1962.

Mr. Greenwood is a member of the Aviation/Space Writers Association and in 1963 was awarded their coveted national trophy for "excellence in promoting public relations in aviation and space activities." He and his wife and two daughters live in Wichita, Kansas, where he works as press relations manager for the Beech Aircraft Corporation—a job that he says is more conducive to longevity than "splitting silk" for Sunday crowds.